AMERICAN EAGLES

RICCARDO NICCOLI

AMERICAN EAGLES

THE GREATEST PHOTOGRAPHS OF THE USAF

CHARTWELL
BOOKS, INC.

Directors:
Marco Drago, Andrea Boroli

Editorial coordinator:
Cristina Cappa Legora

Editorial directors:
Valeria Camaschella

Photographic Coordination
by the Centro Iconografico
of the Istituto Geografico De Agostini
directed by Maria Serena Battaglia

Cover
Marco Volpati

All the photos are by the author except for the following:

USAF: 11, 50, 104, 108 top, 109 top, 111, 113 top,

Department of Defense 16, 78 bottom, 81 top, 90 top;

Kihei Kitagawa 80 top, 136 (VC-25A);

Jyrki Laukkanen 37;

Gianni Gambarini 136 (EC-18B);

Aldo Ciarini 142 (UV-18B)

Published by
CHARTWELL BOOKS, INC.
A Division of BOOK SALES, INC.
114 Northfield Avenue
Edison, New Jersey 08837
Printed by Officine Grafiche De Agostini - Novara 1999
Legatura: Legatoria del Verbano

ISBN 0-7858-1190-7

Contents

For the past half century, the United States Air Force has been responsible for commanding the air and space environment in service to the United States. From the Berlin Airlift in 1947 to today's efforts in Bosnia, the accomplishments recorded by the men and women of the Air Force represent a proud legacy.

During our 50th Anniversary year, we want to highlight the contributions of air power pioneers as well as share the stories of service and sacrifice by all members of the service. We also want to look to the future where we see air and space systems serving in peacetime as well as war. The 21st century will clearly be the age of air and space power.

The legacy of our veterans is a bold, blue line stretching from the pioneering days of aviation into the 21st Century. This year we celebrate the 50 years of hard work and dedication displayed by the thousands of men and women who served their nation in the Air Force. With the past challenges in mind, and remembering the lessons and achievements of the people who built the Air Force, we look forward to a boundless future.

RONALD R. FOGLEMAN
General, USAF
Chief of Staff

INTRODUCTION

A ll those who are fascinated by the magic of flight, and particularly by military flying in aircraft at the apex of performance and technological development, cannot fail to be interested and caught up in the history, operations and equipment of the United States Air Force. This air force, the most powerful and versatile air instrument in the world, embodies in its strength the powers of American aviation: vast capacity, powerful aircraft and high technology.

The USAF, or Air Force, as it is familiarly known to its staff, is an armed force of vast dimensions, with a support organization comprising more than 800,000 men and women, civilians and military, full and part-time, who undertake work in spheres of which many are completely ignored even by the most informed aviation enthusiasts.

Besides the normal activity undertaken by an air force, the fulfilling of the roles of air superiority, bombing, reconnaissance, transport, search and rescue, training, maintenance, and humanitarian missions in favour of populations afflicted by war or natural disasters, the USAF is further occupied in particularly advanced and delicate sectors, such as the management of nuclear weapons, of military operations in space, and of an extensive system of communication, information, research and control.

Moreover, the Air Force has been charged with the task of operating on a global scale, also in support of the other American armed forces, as a long range arm of American military and political power, and coincidentally as an asset of NATO and the United Nations. To this end, it can deploy highly developed transport and in-flight refuelling components, and boasts an advanced and powerful strategic bombing force.

THE ORIGINS

The first considerations in respect of the importance of air power to the United States can be attributed to Benjamin Franklin, who, while in France in 1793, produced some interesting observations on the military possibilities of the use of balloons, having observed the ascents of Jean de Rozier in Paris. There was, however, a delay of many

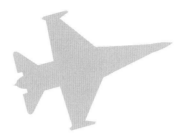

years before the first air service was actually initiated: this was the Balloon Corps of the Army of the Potomac, which was officially inaugurated on June 19th 1861.

It was, however, only on August 1st 1907, with the institution of the Aeronautical Division of the Signal Corps that the American Army was provided with a true and proper military air branch, intended to operate balloons, flying machines, and similar objects: three years had already passed since the first flight of the Wright brothers. James Allen was the first commander of the Aeronautical Division. In August 1909 the US Army put into operation its first aircraft, "Aeroplane Number 1", which was unfortunately lost in an accident some three months later.

Although with less progress than took place in Europe, aviation began to develop in America, and in 1916 the Aviation Section of the Signal Corps undertook its first combat operations, albeit limited to the roles of reconnaissance and observation, when the 1st Aero Squadron, equipped with Curtiss JN-2 and JN-3, was placed at the disposal of General Pershing for the capture of the legendary bandit Pancho Villa. Despite the unsatisfactory results of the campaign, the 1st Aero Squadron, which had lost six of the eight aircraft in charge for various reasons, had however accumulated 346 flying hours in 540 missions.

THE TWO WORLD WARS

One year later, the United States had entered the war in Europe, but the Aviation Section could boast only 35 pilots and some 260 aircraft, none of which were combat-capable. To solve this situation, having to face an enemy equipped with very advanced aircraft, President Wilson signed the Aviation Act, which sanctioned the expenditure of

600 million dollars for the development of military aviation. With this outlay, not only
Aviation Section, but the American aviation industry "took off".

In the light of the technological gap that separated the USA and Europe, it was
decided to equip the combat squadrons with French SPAD and Nieuport fighters,
while the home industries would concentrate on the production of aircraft for
reconnaissance and training. On May 24th 1918, the US Army decided to detach the
air element from the Signal Corps and to create a separate US Army Air Service . The
effects of this updating policy soon became apparent: at the conclusion of the First
World War in November 1918, the USAAS had 195,023 personnel and 7,889 aircraft.

After the war, together with a general demobilization, a great debate arose about
the possibility of elevating the USAAS to an independent status, as had already been
done in Great Britain with the Royal Flying Corps, whose name had been changed to
"Royal Air Force" in 1918. In the debate which took up increasingly heated tones,
Billy Mitchell came to the fore, although he made the mistake of increasingly attacking
the military establishment through the mass media. In 1925 Mitchell was brought
before a Court Martial, found guily and suspended from service for five years.

In the meantime, however, other more discreet activities were suggested in order
to elevate the professionalism and operational capabilities of the service. On July 2nd
1926 Congress approved the Air Corps Act, by which the USAAS was elevated to Corps
level (US Army Air Corps - USAAC) with the possibility of representation in the general
staff: this allowed an increased budget, bringing the force up to 20,000 men and 1,800
aircraft. In 1934 the Baker Board to whom the task of establishing the suitability or
not of a separate air force had been entrusted, answered the question in the negative

An USAFE F-100D taken while landing on an airbase in Europe, at the end of the 1950s.

but recommended the establishment of a separate overall general command for the Air Corps, in order to centralise control over the individual units. The Air Force GHQ was instituted at Langley, Virginia.

In the next few years the attention of the world was focused on European affairs, and on the rising power of Germany. American isolationist feelings were rapidly changing with the growth of the Nazi threat and in the years immediately preceding the Second World War the potential of the USAAC was further increased. In1938 the Air Corps controlled some 21,089 personnel, while within three years the figure had risen to 354,000. At the same time aircraft production, which in June 1940 had been running at 400 aircraft per month, had risen to 2,464 aicraft per month by December 1941.

Thanks to the presence of men of wide vision, such as President Franklin D. Roosevelt and the Army Chief of Staff, General George Marshall, on June 20th 1941 the War Powers Act, which permitted, amongst other things, the creation of the US. Army Air Forces (USAAF) as an autonomous air arm, although not completely independent, was signed. The Commander of the USAAF, General Henry H. Arnold, could thereby obtain by right a place amongst the Joint Chiefs of Staff and the Allied Combined Chiefs of Staff.

When on December 7th 1941 the United States entered the war, the USAAF commenced operations on various theatres from the Pacific to Europe and in the Middle East, more and more increasing the numbers of men and machines in service. The campaigns of the Second World War are too well documented and too complex to be quoted and described here: it is sufficient to record that during the war years the Service reached unparalleled operational dimensions. In 1944 some 2,370,000 men and women and 78,757 aircraft were distributed amongst 16 Air Forces.

THE BIRTH OF THE USAF

Thanks also to the convictions of General Dwight D. Eisenhower, at the end of the war the time was right for the institution of a really and truly independent air force, a process that was gradually achieved thanks to a general and radical reorganization that involved all the American armed forces. On July 27th 1947 President Harry S. Truman, on board a C- 54 of the USAAF, signed the National Security Act, merging the two Ministry Department (War and Navy) into one Department, the Department of Defence, which controlled as subdepartments the three armed forces: Army, Navy and Air Force.

The new US Air Force (USAF) was officially created on September 18th 1947, and its first Chief of Staff was General Carl A. Spaatz. Executive order 9877 established the missions assigned to the USAF: to organize, train and equip air forces for global and theatre level air superiority, for strategic combat, reconnaissance and air transport; to develop weapons and tactics; to prepare, plan and undertake missions on a global scale in pursuance of national and political interests; to coordinate air-defence missions and to assist and support, if necessary, the Army and Navy. The latter service retained full control of its own air assets, while the Army could operate a fleet of light transports and helicopters for tactical observation and transport.

The Air Force was still in the midst of major development when, on June 25th 1950, the Korean War broke out. It was the era of transition between propeller and jet aicraft, and in 1950 the USAF found itself in possession of a force of 16,857 aircraft, but in less

than three years the total had risen to 24,918. Although the Korean conflict was by no means a resounding military success, the Air Force activities were positive, with a favourable combat success ratio and successful ground attack and short and long range transport operations.

TOWARDS A GLOBAL AIR POWER

The 1950s saw the USAF firmly established at the head of the air forces of the world, first and foremost on a technical and strategic level. The aviation industry, in conjuncion with the air force, produced on a large scale a wide range of advanced and mass produced aircraft which were going to become famous throughout the world, such as the B-52 and the SR-71 still performing validly today. Moreover, the crucial period of the Cold War forced the USAF to pay particular attention to its strategic forces, called on to be able to strike the Soviet Union territory quicky and efficiently, if need be, in response to a nuclear attack.

The Sixties and the early Seventies are remembered mainly for the unfortunate Vietnam War, in which the American armed forces were heavily and lengthily involved but in which, for various reasons, they were unable to achieve results proportionate to the technical, economic and human endeavour that was expended.

In the 1970s, the USAF continued to expand its presence in Space activity. It also made continued progress on satellite-based communications, reconnaissance, warning, weather, and navigation systems. Meanwhile, rapid progress was being made in new technologies, such as "stealthy" airframes, and sophisticated information

networks.

Since those days, and until today, the USAF has undergone a slow and progressive reduction in the size of its forces. On the one hand, technological progress has made available aircraft more and more complex, costly and capable to provide results superior to what had been achieved in the past with larger numbers. On the other hand, a constant reduction in the forces, apart from the presidential term of Ronald Reagan, has been necessary to meet budgetary problems which, with the collapse of the Berlin Wall, have concurred with the virtual disappearance of the USA's principal political and military opponent: the USSR.

As the military potential of the Warsaw Pact evaporated, the American armed forces underwent a gradual but consistent reduction in staff, equipment and bases, both in America and overseas. Moreover at the start of the 1990s, the structure of the USAF was reorganized, which brought to the disappearance of some of the traditional Commands, such as Tactical Air Command, Strategic Air Command, Military Airlift Command, Air Force Systems Command and Logistic Command, giving rise to the present structure described in this book.

The end of the present century has witnessed the USAF play a major role in the new peace-keeping missions approved and organized under the aegis of the United Nations: the Gulf War against Iraq and the subsequent surveillance operations; the mission in Somalia; air operations over the former Jugoslavia, beginning with the Deny Flight operation: we all have seen the massive use of combat and support units of the USAF, all of which have amply demonstrated their effectiveness. Once again, the USAF

The F-4 *Phantom* was the prime fighter aircraft during the Vietnam War. This F-4D from the 8th TFW is ready for a bombing mission over North Vietnam at the beginning of the 1970s.

15

An element of F-15E from 48th FW in-flight over the Adriatic Sea during Operation "Deny Flight" on the former Yugoslavia.

has displayed its excellent operational capabilities in the difficult field of the projection of force, the potential to deploy major combat units over intercontinental distances and to replenish them during their operations.

It is always difficult to predict what the future will hold. If politics, philosophies and strategic and tactical priorities can change with time, there is no doubt that the existence of a significant autonomous air power like the USAF, equipped with first rate staff and means, able to engage in any type of military aviation activity on a global scale, will always be a guarantee of freedom and independence for the people of the United States and for their friends.

Due to the limited space of this book, the subject of this photo-album is confined to the mere operational flying component of the US Air Force, the more spectacular and admired by the public. Therefore, with much regret, all the units and agencies operating in the technical, logistical and administrative field have been excluded, as well as the Air Education and Training Command and the Air Force Space Command, which indeed deserve dedicated publications.

Apologizing for this forced omission, we feel it our duty in this context to mention and appreciate the work and the professionality of all the USAF personnel, without any exceptions.

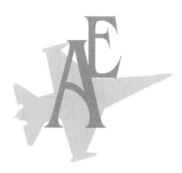

FOTOALBUM

FIGHTERS

*F*ighters have always been considered the "star" category in military aviation. Whether we consider these aircraft designed to attain air superiority or to fly at low level, striking the enemy well inside its territory, fighters have always been the state of the art of technology, the most powerful and highly perfected flying machines at the disposal of mankind. The missions assigned to these aircraft are various and all equally indispensable. The F-15A and C *Eagles* destined to carry out air defence, air superiority and interception missions, in spite of their age, are still able to provide top level performances as far as flight qualities, mission equipment and armament are concerned. The *Eagles* whose task it is to clear the sky from enemy aircraft, must insure the necessary security to attack fighters: the F-15E *Strike Eagles*, the F-16C *Fighting Falcons*, the F-117A *Nighthawks* and the A/OA-10A *Thunderbolt II*. Modern fighterbombers are developing more and more as multirole fighters, capable of excellent performances even in the air-to-air scenario. This is the case for the F-15E and the F-16C, which can be armed and operated for attack and air combat tasks at the same time. The F-117, also known as *Stealth Fighter, or Black Jet*, represents, on the contrary, a technological effort to attain the maximum "invisibility" on the battlefield: it does not have multirole capability, but only the task of high precision bombing on very important targets. Finally the A-10 is a fighter-bomber dedicated to Close Air Support and observation in favour of ground forces. Given the capability of these aircraft, the human component is more important than ever.

An F-15E *Strike Eagle* of the 4th FW taken at take-off.

To fly at 600 mph, a few feet above the ground, often at night or in bad weather; to engage in aerial combat manoeuvres which subject the body to as much as 9G; to manage instantly the keyboard of sophisticated electronic systems, interactive multifunction screens, night vision devices, while flying on the edge, represents a more and more difficult challenge for modern fighter pilots.

Today more than ever, the Air Force fighter crews, destined to carry out their missions in the world, from the Alaskan ice to the Arabian deserts, from the seas of the Far East to the forests of Europe, ready to move on call to fly under the United States, NATO or UN flags, must excel in individual skills, combined with a strict top-level continuous training.

And the arrival on the scene of the latest and most advanced "superfighter", the F-22 *Raptor* is looming on the horizon.

The F-15 *Eagle*, A or C version, is the USAF air superiority fighter. Each F-15 Fighter Wing is composed by a number of Squadron, usually one to three, each of them equipped with 18 or 24 aircraft.

1. An F-15A from the 131st FW, Missouri ANG, taken during a looping.

2. The pilot's view inside the cockpit of an F-15 *Eagle*.

3. A simple gesture witnesses the care of the maintenance personnel for their aircraft.

4. An F-15 pilot taken after a combat training mission.

3

2

4

On the preceding page:
F-15 flight line on the base
at Tyndall AFB, Florida, during
a "William Tell" exercise.

1. Taken inside a hardened
shelter at Aviano AB, Italy,
this USAFE F-15C, equipped
with three external fuel
tanks, and AIM-7, AIM-9,
and AIM-120 missiles,
awaits its next mission during
the NATO operation
on the former Yugoslavia.

2. Pilots and technicians
check an aircraft before
its mission. They always
perform a team work.

2

3

3. Taken at the take-off
from Nellis AFB, Nevada,
this F-15E *Strike Eagles*
belongs to the 57th Wing.

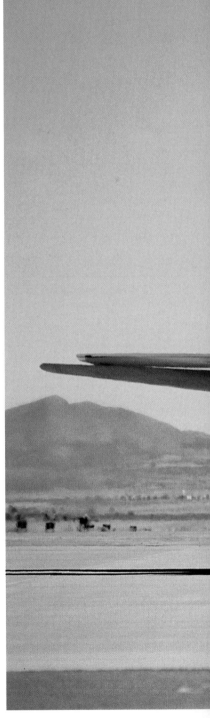

1. An F-15E crew of the 53rd Wing taken before take-off. Crew coordination is everything in the *Strike Eagle*.

2

2. Pilots and WSO of the 4th FW while planning a mission. The briefing and de-briefing activities play a major role in the modern air operations.

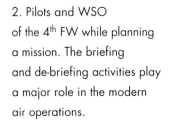

3. An F-15E of 366th Wing taken while taxiing.

On the next page: the dawn lights up the *Strike Eagles* on the flight line at Nellis AFB.

F-16C *Fighting Falcons* of 388th FW taken during a take-off in pairs. The F-16 is the most numerous aircraft in the USAF inventory.

1

1. A pilot checks some
practice bombs during
a "Gunsmoke" exercise.

2. Taken in-flight, this F-16D
from the 347th Wing
is the two-seater training model
of the *Fighting Falcon*.

2

1. Pilot and crew-chief of an F-16A ADF of North Dakota ANG taken during the last checks before a mission.

2. Close-up on the camouflaged tail of an F-16C "aggressor" of the 57th Wing.

3. Full-AB take-off from the Richmond airport for this F-16C of the 192nd FW, Virginia ANG.

4. During an in-flight refuelling operation, this F-16 pilot has anyway the time to show that "everything is OK".

1

3

SrA Jason Owens

4

The F-117A *Nighthawk* is for sure the most unusual and mysterious fighterbomber in the USAF history. Its squared aerodynamics assure good "invisibility" to the enemy radar, but poor flight agility.

On the preceding page, an F-16C of 56th FW in-flight over the Arizona desert.

Two A/OA-10A *Thunderbolt II* of the 57th Wing, loaded with Mk.82 bombs, are ready to take-off from the Nellis runway. The most impressive weapon of the *Thunderbolt II* is its Gatling GAU-8 gun (left), featured by seven 30mm barrells, which is long nearly half the fusolage.

1

1. An A/OA-10A in flight
in the Nevada skies shows its
high ordnance load capability,
thanks to its numerous
underwing hardpoints,
and also the positioning
of its engines, partly protected
and shielded by the wing
and the tail planes.

2. Today a "must" for night
operations, the Night Vision
Goggles (NVG) allow pilots
to fly safely and effectively
during night combat missions.

3. An A/OA-10A taxies
to the take-off.

2

3

BOMBERS

*I*n a world where military technology is becoming more and more costly, and where specialised aircraft are sacrificed in favour of multi-role machines, capable of performing various missions, the USAF is still able to deploy dedicated strategic bombers, aircraft studied expressly to fly long distances and deliver heavy warloads, including nuclear weapons.

The B-2A *Spirit* is certainly the most expensive and fascinating aircraft in the entire Air Force fleet. A "flying wing" of futuristic design, looking almost like an escapee from a science fiction movie, the B-2A is the maximum technological expression of "invisible flight" able to leave, despite its dimensions, a minimum radar trace, thanks to its accurate design, its component materials and the paints in which it is finished. Its navigational and attack systems are equally advanced, to the point that the crew required to manage this "superior aircraft" consists of only two people: pilot and navigator.

The B-1B *Lancer*, however, is a more conventional bomber, where the compromise between invisibility and performance is much more accentuated. Nevertheless, its operational capabilities remain exceptional, such that the *Lancer*, able to carry up to around 56 tonnes of bombs or missiles, remains the backbone of the strategic bomber force and, thanks to its variable geometry wing, is the only big bomber capable of supersonic speed and good manoeuvrability.

Finally, to complete this "triad", comes the tireless B-52 *Stratofortress*, which for more than thirty-five years has symbolised American air power. With its imposing size, its eight engines and over 22 tonnes of warloads, the *Stratofortress* has seen service in all the wars and crises that have arisen from the Vietnam war to the Gulf war, having passed successfully through several fleet renewal programmes which were threatening its end. Still today, even though technologically outdated, the B-52 continuously upgraded in its components, still remains a valid aircraft in the USAF inventory.

As opposed to fighter-bombers, agile and fast attack aircraft, bombers represent a different operational philosophy, being designed to strike targets of strategic value at long distances, often with missiles that can be launched at long range from their intended targets. The bombers' defence remains above all based on their elecronic self-defence capability and their crews, used to flying missions of 10 or 15 hours, are men with nerves of steel and solid training, called on to operate in the delicate sphere of nuclear weapons with the utmost professionalism and safety.

A B-52H during in-flight refuelling.

The menacing and futuristic outline of this B-2 *Spirit* of the 509th BW well emerges from this view.

Either on the ground or in flight, the B-2 has an extraordinary outlook. Due to its huge costs, caused by the advanced technologies, even the USAF could purchase only twenty of them.

A B-1B *Lancer* of the 366th
Wing taken at the take-off
from Nellis AFB, the base
which is the heart of the USAF
combat training.

One of the main features of the B-1B is its swing wing, which allows surprising performances. The B-1B is in service with three Wings: at Dyess AFB, Texas; at Ellsworth AFB, South Dakota; at Mountain Home AFB, Idaho.

1

1. Loading operations
on the B-1B are long
and meticolous: the *Lancer* can
carry up to 84 Mk.82 bombs.

2. The B-1B is a quite
big aircraft: its impressive
tail is over ten meters
high from the ground.

Here and on the preceding page: the B-52H, an aircraft with a long operational history, is still in service with two units: the 2nd BW at Barksdale AFB, Louisiana, and the 5th BW at Minot AFB, North Dakota.

RECONNAISSANCE AND SPECIAL MISSION

*T*he march of technological development, above all in the field of electronics, has changed not only everyday human life, but also and above all the operational necessities of air forces. Missions and tasks that in the past were neglected or inexistent, are today considered indispensable for the successful outcome of air operations. Above all, this concerns the roles of optical and electronic reconnaissance at both tactical and strategic level, and the duties of radar and electronic surveillance (ELINT-SIGINT), communication, command and control (C3) and electronic warfare (ECM-ESM). In these sectors, the USAF employs the widest and most complete range of aircraft in the world, able to cover the different requirements of commands, and to supply in an accurate and rapid manner the fundamental element of a modern conflict: information.

From the incredible SR-71 *Blackbird*, capable of flying at an altitude of 24,000 m (about 80,000 ft) at 3,500 km/h (2,000 miles per hour), and of surveying more than 259,000 Km^2 of territory in one hour, to the "peaceful" EC-130H *Compass Call* electronic warfare aircraft, which can superimpose its own electronic emissions over those of an enemy, rendering any type of tactical and strategic communications impossible, the USAF is currently able to deploy an impressive range of aircraft dedicated to these specific tasks.

For strategic reconnaissance there are the U-2, the SR-71 and the RC-135; available for C3 are E-8, E-3, E-4, E-9, EC-135, and EC-130 and finally, for electronic warfare a few EC-130 and the EF-111 are operational.

As is apparent, high performance aircraft are not generally necessary for these types of mission, but reliable aircraft, with good cargo capacity, able to fly at high altitude at subsonic speeds over long distances are well -suited; they must carry sophisticated electronic systems and a large crew. Many of these aircraft are derived from commercial airliners, such as the Boeing 747 or 707. The men on board these aircraft are, each in their own field, specialists, whose characteristic are not the aggressiveness and physical strength of combat pilots, but a deep technical knowledge of electronics and operational systems. Tasked to perform very long and tiring mission, they must be prepared to control difficult aircraft such as the U-2 or the SR 71, piloting inside their unconfortable pressurized flying suites; or to work at computers and radar screens, real technicians who, at an altitude of 10,000 m (30,000 ft) or more, wear a flying suit instead of the laboratory white coats.

RECONNAISSANCE AND SPECIAL MISSION

Here and on the preceding page: the SR-71 *Blackbird*, at about forty years from its maiden flight still is an aircraft with extraordinary features and performances. Three examples are in service with the 9th RW at the Edwards AFB, California.

1. The U-2S reconnaissance aircraft is a vital mean for the gathering of datas and information. In the future it will be replaced by UAVs.

2. An U-2 pilot walks to his aircraft. This kind of pressurized flying suite, which costs about 150,000 dollars, is worn also by the SR-71 pilots in all the high altitude flights.

Photos 1, 3 and on the preceding page: the E-3C AWACS for command and control operations is the aircraft capable to surveille and monitor huge airspace areas, and to manage the flight operations of many other aircraft. The "heart" of the AWACS is its radar system, whose large rotating antenna is positioned above the fusolage.

2. Operators at work on the control screens of an E-3C.

1

2

3

1. An RC-135V *Rivet Joint III* for electronic reconnaissance of the 55th Wing landing at Kadena, in Japan.

2. An EF-111A for Electronic Warfare from the 27th FW taken in flight over the Rocky Mountains.

3. The EW-ECM role for the USAF is being transferred from the EF-111A to the EA-6B *Prowler* of the US Navy. Some units already fly with mixed USAF-US Navy crews, as witnessed by this aircraft of the VAQ-142.

2

AIRLIFT AND TANKERS

The transport and in-flight refuelling component of an air force is often less considered and appreciated than other spheres, perhaps more interesting and striking, such as "fighting"

However the prompt operational capability of the USAF and of the American armed forces in general, on a global scale, depends to a large extent on the successful functioning of the units dedicated to transport and in-flight refuelling. These units are, in fact, the ones that permit the rapid deployment, even over intercontinental distances, of not only combat aircraft, accompanied by their personnel and support equipment, but also of supplies, troops, vehicles, including even helicopters and armoured fighting vehicles for the other armed forces - above all the US Army - and of all the equipment useful or indispensable in an operational theatre different to and distant from the usual bases. The recent scenario of the Gulf war was emblematic. The in-flight refuelling aircraft, real force multipliers, by now enable all aircraft, both combat and support, to remain longer over the area of operations or to undertake non-stop intercontinental flights, a type of mission that now represents normal operations for the units of the USAF.

The heavy transport component is primarily constituted by the C-5 *Galaxy* and C-141 *Starlifter*, which have recently been joined by the new C-17 *Globemaster III*: all these heavyweight four-engined, large capacity aircraft are specifically designed to undertake military roles. Other aircraft, derived from commercial models, are dedicated to the transport of passengers and fright with lesser or different load capacities: these are the C-9, C-12, C-20, C-21 and C-22, while the VC-25 are entrusted with Presidential transport. Tactical transport is entrusted to the popular and reliable C-130 *Hercules*, to the fleet of which the new C-130J will shortly be added. The USAF tanker fleet consists mainly of the KC-135 *Stratotanker*, of which more than 500 examples remain operational (they are the fourth most numerous type in service after F-16, F-15 and C-130), which are assisted by the more modern KC-10 *Extender*.

A C-17A of the 437th AW, based at Charleston AFB, South Carolina.

The C-5B *Galaxy* is the "heavy-weight" in service with the USAF. The 120 and more examples in use are mainly distributed between the 60th AMW, at Travis AFB, California, and the 436th AW, at Dover AFB, Delaware.

On the next page, a C-5B gently lands on the base at Travis, while another aircraft of the same type waits the clearance to take-off.

3. Even if apparently "bulkier" and smaller than the C-141, the C-17A is capable to carry double the load of a *Starlifter*.

4. The advanced aerodynamics features of the C-17A can be used to create strange photographic tricks.

Photos 1 and 2. The C-141B *Starlifter*, in service in more than 200 examples, is the "backbone" of the USAF strategic transportation capability. After more than 30 years of service, it is currently being replaced by the C-17A.

3

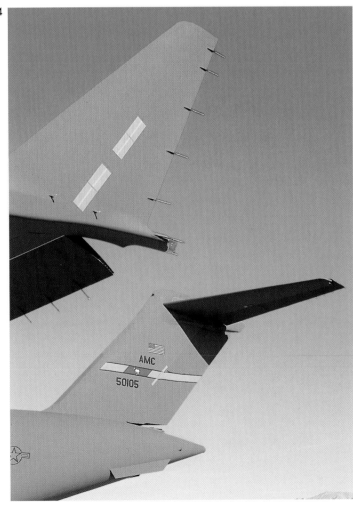

4

1. The big mass of the C-17A is clearly visible from this view.

2. A KC-10 tanker taken at dawn, in the moonlight, on one of the ramps at Travis.

3. A KC-10 crew discuss its mission postflight.

3

Photos 1 and 2. Two faces of the same coin: the in-flight refuelling of KC-10s from the boom operator position (left) and from the cockpit (right).

2

3

3. The boom operator position. Down through the window it is possible to see an F-16C receiving its fuel.

1

2

3

On the preceding page:
KC-135 pilots at work
during a mission.

1. Line-up of tails of KC-135E
from the 108th ARW, New
Jersey ANG. Under the tails
it is possible to see the in-flight
refuelling booms.

2. The KC-135 is a military
model of the famous Boeing 707.

3. Wonderful artwork
on the nose of this
KC-135 belonging to
the New Jersey "tigers".

The C-130 *Hercules* is "the" tactical trasport of the USAF, but it is used also for other important roles, as the fire-fighting, witnessed by the photo on the right.

HELICOPTERS AND SPECIAL OPERATIONS

There are not many helicopters in service with the USAF, and in the main they are employed in minor liason and transport tasks (UH-1 and HH-1). However. a part of the fleet consists of highly sophisticated machines, which are used by AFSOC in support of Special Operations. A few models of the C-130 still operate in this field, often with little publicity: thanks to major conversion programmes, they can be employed in a vast range of missions on behalf of the Special Operation Command.

The sphere of Special Operations brings together under one classification differing types of missions which in substance are those that can be described as "unconventional warfare", a type of activity that in recent times has taken up an even greater importance. To this kind belong discreet insertion and evacuation by night of special combat units, or long range reconnaissance in hostile or enemy territory, fire support for these missions, in-flight refuelling over enemy territory, search and rescue of personnel missing in enemy territory (Combat- SAR), electronic and psychological warfare operations, and anti-terrorism duties.

The crews of this aircraft are not only qualified pilots and crewmen, but possess, in addition, the psycho-physical characteristics and training of the special forces, capable of operating in critical situations, often nearly isolated in hostile environments, using weapons and supplies more typical of ground forces than of flying crews.

An AC-130H "gunship" flying over the Gulf of Mexico.

The helicopters used by AFSOC are the agile MH-60 *Pave Hawk* and the heavy MH-53 *Pave Low*, both equipped with advanced navigation and self-defence systems, including armament for their own defence and for the support of ground forces; they are used for the transport and evacuation of personnel. The airplanes are the MC-130 *Combat Talon*, and the HC-130 *Combat Shadow*, tasked with transporting troops and supplies, and with paradrops, in-flight refuelling of helicopters and even with the delivery of special bombs such as the enormous BLU-82. There are also the AC-130 *Spectre*, virtually flying gunships, armed with artillery guns of various calibre coupled with sophisticated sensors and computers capable of directing a stream of projectiles surgically onto any chosen target. Finally, there are EC-130 E *Commando Solo* electronic warfare aircraft, which can syperimpose their own colour television transmission over the frequences of those of an enemy broadcast, performing an important mission of psychological warfare against the public opinion of an hostile country.

0512

DCC C COUPENS
ACC B KASPER

The AC-130U *Spectre* is the latest type of gunship operated by the USAF. It flies with the 16th SOW at Hurlburt Field AFB, Florida, and it is equipped with sophisticated fire control systems.

1

2

Photos 1, 2, 3, 4. The Special
Operation Forces of the USAF
operate several types
of C-130 *Hercules* for training
or for operational use.
On the right, (photos 3 and 4)
two views of MC-130H,
the model destined to fly
and penetrate inside the enemy
territory at night and/or in bad
weather conditions.

3

4

5

5.Two crew members
of a AC-130H gunship show
the ammunitions destined
to the 40mm and 105mm guns
firing from the port side of
the aircraft. These are weapons
destined to the suppression
of enemy ground forces.

1. Clear from this view
the peculiar set of antennas
featuring the tail of this
EC-130E "Commando Solo"
of the 193rd SOW.

2

1

2. In-flight refuelling between MH-60G helicopters and an HC-130P of the Special Operation Forces.

Photos 1 and 2. MH-60G
Pave Hawk helicopters taken
in-action. The team
for Combat-SAR operations
is formed by two aircraft.

2

3. A heavy helicopter MH-53J
Pave Low III in-flight low
level in a typical operational
environment.

3

U.S. AIR FORCE

50

1947 - 1997

THE 50th ANNIVERSARY

DANGER
DANGER DANGER

A/C CAPT STEVE RITCHIE
WSO CAPT CHUCK DEBELLEVUE
C/C SGT REGINALD TAYLOR

RESCUE

Brig Gen Steve Ritchie

Maj Vinnie Farrell

AIR COMBAT COMMAND

*R*eaching fifty years of activity represents an important moment for any organisation, public or private. After the work of half a century, a moment of reflection an rejoicing is necessary, to celebrate what has been done and to continue with renewed vigour in order to meet what is to come. This holds true in the world of aviation, where fifty years are full of both glorious and tragic memories, and where moments of personal and collective joy are as intense as the moments of sadness which, in peace and wartime, despite all best efforts, inexorably occur.

Naturally, the roots of the USAF run much deeper than the fifty years that are celebrated during 1997, but the date of 18th September 1947 represents a fundamental and unforgettable day for all the men and women who wear the blue uniform.

Among the many official air displays held at many USAF airbases, the one we have chosen to document as a symbol of all the celebrations is the *Golden Air Tattoo*, held at Nellis AFB (Las Vegas), on April 25th and 26th 1997. On this occasion, in fact, in the splendid scenery of the American West, which for many symbolises the myth of the Frontier, the Air Force has presented to the public – more than 400,000 persons – all its past and present. The flying display of the *Thunderbids* USAF aerobatic team and of the fighters and bombers of 2000 were mixed with their forebears, protagonists in historical events and conflicts which in the past have witnessed the commitments of the United States Air Force on many fronts throughout the globe. On the ground, in a static display before the public, were drawn up all the aircraft that have seen service throughout the years, together with the aircraft of friendly nations, also invited to join in the grand celebration of the air.

1. The Douglas DC-3, in its military C-47 model, was one of the most important means used by the allied forces in WWII. This is the C-41 of gen. Arnold, commander of the Army Air Force during the war; it was the first military DC-3 ever produced.

2. The P-47 *Thunderbolt* was the main USAAF fighterbomber in WWII.

3. By most, the P-51 *Mustang* was considered the best fighter aircraft of WWII.

4. The B-17 "Flying Fortress" was the main heavy bomber of the USAAF in Europe.

5. The B-25 Mitchell was author of the famous raid over Tokyo, in April 1942.

1

2

3

4

5

1. The T-33 was the first and most popular jet training aircraft in the world.

2. The F-86 was the most advanced fighter aircraft in the Korean War and killed 792 MiGs in the three-years period of the conflict.

APPENDIX

USAF STRUCTURE

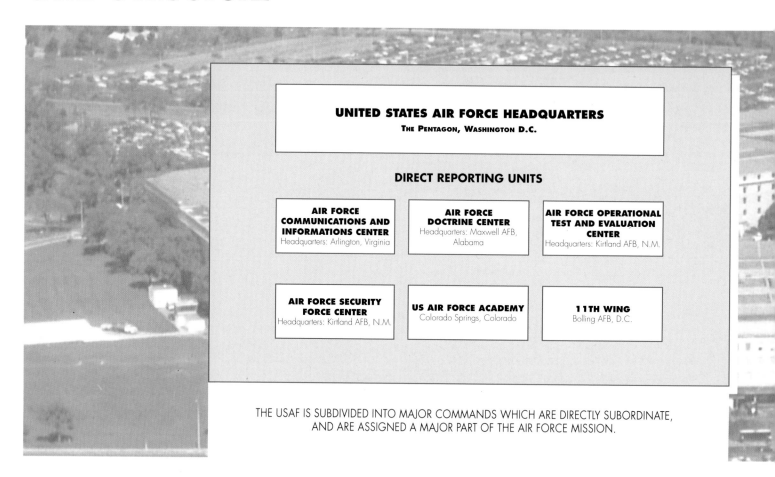

UNITED STATES AIR FORCE HEADQUARTERS
The Pentagon, Washington D.C.

DIRECT REPORTING UNITS

AIR FORCE COMMUNICATIONS AND INFORMATIONS CENTER Headquarters: Arlington, Virginia	AIR FORCE DOCTRINE CENTER Headquarters: Maxwell AFB, Alabama	AIR FORCE OPERATIONAL TEST AND EVALUATION CENTER Headquarters: Kirtland AFB, N.M.
AIR FORCE SECURITY FORCE CENTER Headquarters: Kirtland AFB, N.M.	US AIR FORCE ACADEMY Colorado Springs, Colorado	11TH WING Bolling AFB, D.C.

THE USAF IS SUBDIVIDED INTO MAJOR COMMANDS WHICH ARE DIRECTLY SUBORDINATE, AND ARE ASSIGNED A MAJOR PART OF THE AIR FORCE MISSION.

ACC

The ACC operates bombers, combat fighter and attack aircraft; organize, train, equip and maintain combat-ready forces; provide nuclear-capable forces for US Strategic Command. Other activities include monitoring and interception of illegal drug traffic, test of the new combat equipment, of supply aircraft to other regional commands, provide air defence forces to NORAD, operate some air mobility forces in support of US Transportation Command.

The ACC operates B-1, B-2, B-52, F-15, F-16, A/OA-10, F-117, EF-111, SR-71, U-2, C-27, and other minor types of aircraft distributed between 25 Wings of the active forces. It controls several units of the AFRC and ANG.

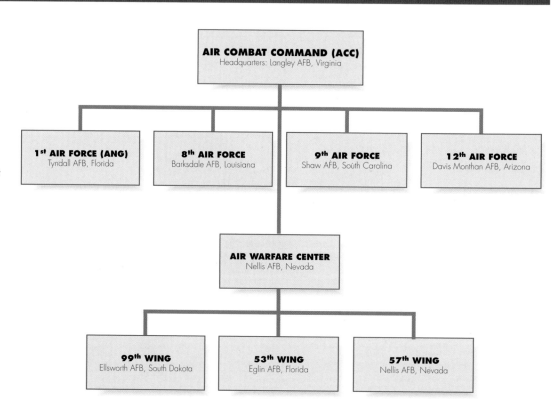

AIR COMBAT COMMAND (ACC)
Headquarters: Langley AFB, Virginia

1st AIR FORCE (ANG)
Tyndall AFB, Florida

8th AIR FORCE
Barksdale AFB, Louisiana

9th AIR FORCE
Shaw AFB, South Carolina

12th AIR FORCE
Davis Monthan AFB, Arizona

AIR WARFARE CENTER
Nellis AFB, Nevada

99th WING
Ellsworth AFB, South Dakota

53rd WING
Eglin AFB, Florida

57th WING
Nellis AFB, Nevada

AMC

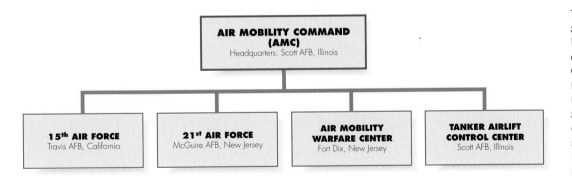

AIR MOBILITY COMMAND (AMC)
Headquarters: Scott AFB, Illinois

15th AIR FORCE
Travis AFB, California

21st AIR FORCE
McGuire AFB, New Jersey

AIR MOBILITY WARFARE CENTER
Fort Dix, New Jersey

TANKER AIRLIFT CONTROL CENTER
Scott AFB, Illinois

The AMC provides rapid, global airlift and aerial refuelling for US Armed Forces; serves as USAF component of US Transportation Command; supports wartime taskings by providing forces to theater commands. Other activities include the providing of operational support aircraft, stateside aeromedical evacuation missions, visual documentation support.

The AMC operates C-5, C-17, C-141, KC-10, KC-135, C-9, C-12, C-20, C-21, VC-9, VC-25, VC-137, UH-1 aircraft distributed between 12 Wings. It controls several units of theAFRC and ANG.

PACAF

The PACAF is assigned the task to plan, conduct and coordinate offensive and defensive air operations in the Pacific and Asian theaters. It also trains, equips and maintains resources to conduct air operations.

The PACAF operates F-15, F-16, A/OA-10, E-3, KC-135, C-9, C-12, C-21, C-130, UH-1, and HH-60 aircraft distributed into 9 Wings.

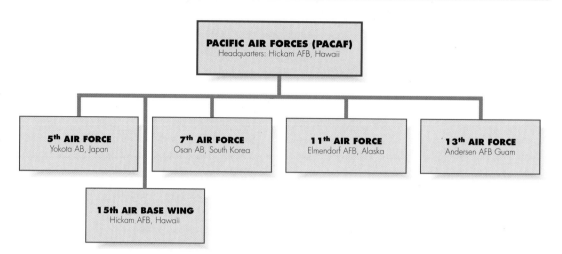

PACIFIC AIR FORCES (PACAF)
Headquarters: Hickam AFB, Hawaii

5th AIR FORCE
Yokota AB, Japan

7th AIR FORCE
Osan AB, South Korea

11th AIR FORCE
Elmendorf AFB, Alaska

13th AIR FORCE
Andersen AFB Guam

15th AIR BASE WING
Hickam AFB, Hawaii

USAFE

The USAFE assigned mission is to plan, conduct, control, coordinate, and support air and space operations to fulfill US and NATO objectives assigned by the Commander-in-Chief of US European Command. It also supports military operations taking place in the Mediterranean, Africa, and the Middle East. In wartime, the USAFE is integrated into NATO forces, under the Allied Command Europe (ACE).

The USAFE operates F-15, F-16, A/OA-10, C-9, C-20, C-21, C-130, KC-135, T-43, MC-130, HC-130, MH-53, and other aircraft deployed to Europe, distributed between 6 Wings.

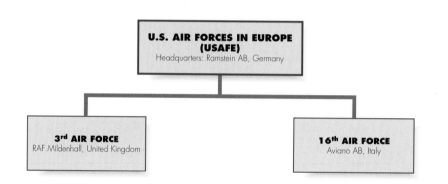

U.S. AIR FORCES IN EUROPE (USAFE)
Headquarters: Ramstein AB, Germany

3rd AIR FORCE
RAF Mildenhall, United Kingdom

16th AIR FORCE
Aviano AB, Italy

AETC

The AETC assigned mission consist of the recruiting, assessment, training, and education of enlisted and officer personnel. It provides various training activities, and also recalls individual ready reservists, supporting combatant commands.

The AETC operates F-15, F-16, C-5, C-141, KC-135, AT/T-38, T-1, T-3, T-37, T-43, C-21, HC-130, MC-130, MH/TH-53, UH-1, MH-60 aircraft, distributed between 10 Wings and other minor units.

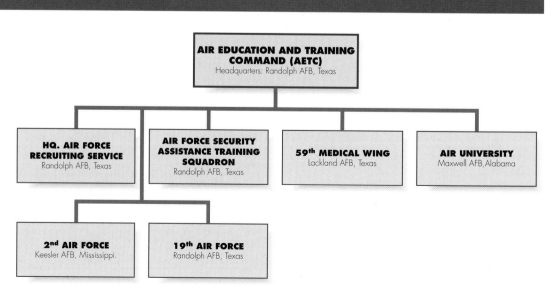

AIR EDUCATION AND TRAINING COMMAND (AETC)
Headquarters: Randolph AFB, Texas

HQ. AIR FORCE RECRUITING SERVICE
Randolph AFB, Texas

AIR FORCE SECURITY ASSISTANCE TRAINING SQUADRON
Randolph AFB, Texas

59th MEDICAL WING
Lackland AFB, Texas

AIR UNIVERSITY
Maxwell AFB, Alabama

2nd AIR FORCE
Keesler AFB, Mississippi.

19th AIR FORCE
Randolph AFB, Texas

AFMC

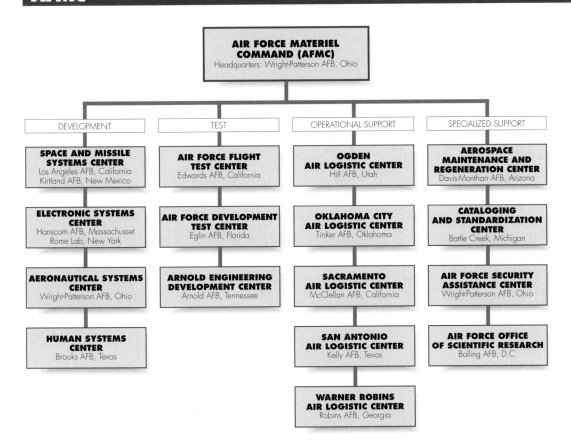

AIR FORCE MATERIEL COMMAND (AFMC)
Headquarters: Wright-Patterson AFB, Ohio

DEVELOPMENT

SPACE AND MISSILE SYSTEMS CENTER
Los Angeles AFB, California
Kirtland AFB, New Mexico

ELECTRONIC SYSTEMS CENTER
Hanscom AFB, Massachusset
Rome Lab, New York

AERONAUTICAL SYSTEMS CENTER
Wright-Patterson AFB, Ohio

HUMAN SYSTEMS CENTER
Brooks AFB, Texas

TEST

AIR FORCE FLIGHT TEST CENTER
Edwards AFB, California

AIR FORCE DEVELOPMENT TEST CENTER
Eglin AFB, Florida

ARNOLD ENGINEERING DEVELOPMENT CENTER
Arnold AFB, Tennessee

OPERATIONAL SUPPORT

OGDEN AIR LOGISTIC CENTER
Hill AFB, Utah

OKLAHOMA CITY AIR LOGISTIC CENTER
Tinker AFB, Oklahoma

SACRAMENTO AIR LOGISTIC CENTER
McClellan AFB, California

SAN ANTONIO AIR LOGISTIC CENTER
Kelly AFB, Texas

WARNER ROBINS AIR LOGISTIC CENTER
Robins AFB, Georgia

SPECIALIZED SUPPORT

AEROSPACE MAINTENANCE AND REGENERATION CENTER
Davis-Monthan AFB, Arizona

CATALOGING AND STANDARDIZATION CENTER
Battle Creek, Michigan

AIR FORCE SECURITY ASSISTANCE CENTER
Wright-Patterson AFB, Ohio

AIR FORCE OFFICE OF SCIENTIFIC RESEARCH
Bolling AFB, D.C.

The AFMC assigned mission is to manage the integrated research, development, test, acquisition and support of weapon systems. It produces and acquires advanced equipment, operates test, logistic, production centers and laboratories, in addition to the USAF Test Pilot School and the USAF School of Aerospace Medicine. It controls 20 units.

AFSPC

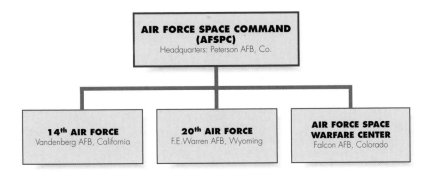

AIR FORCE SPACE COMMAND (AFSPC)
Headquarters: Peterson AFB, Co.

14th AIR FORCE
Vandenberg AFB, California

20th AIR FORCE
F.E. Warren AFB, Wyoming

AIR FORCE SPACE WARFARE CENTER
Falcon AFB, Colorado

The AFSPC is the major command assigned to operate ICBM forces for the US Strategic Command, worldwide space surveillance radars and optical systems, missile warning radars, satellites, and other sensors. It operates also bases and facilities for space and missile launches. It provides ballistic missile warning and command and control for military satellites, and military space operations. The Commander of AFSPC is also Commander-in-Chief of NORAD and US Space Command.
The AFSPC operates Minuteman III and Peacekeeper ICBMs plus several satellite systems and boosters. It controls 7 Wings and 4 Groups.

AFSOC

The AFSOC is the Air Force component of the US Special Operations Command. It is tasked to deploy anytime, anywhere in the world to provide specialized airpower and to deliver special operations.
Its specialization are unconventional warfare, special reconnaissance, counterterrorism, foreign internal defence, humanitarian assistance, psycological operations, personnel recovery, counternarcotics operations.
It operates AC/MC/HC/EC-130, MH-53, MH-60 aircraft

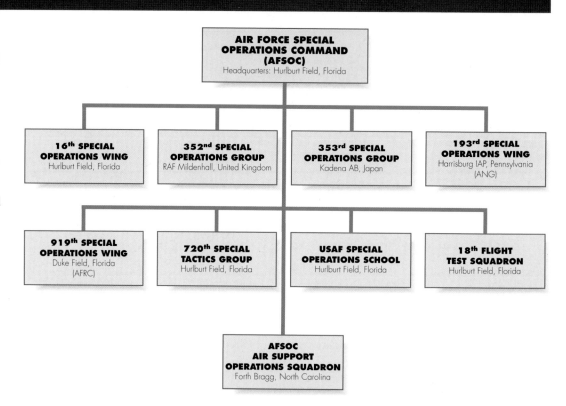

AIR FORCE SPECIAL OPERATIONS COMMAND (AFSOC)
Headquarters: Hurlburt Field, Florida

16th SPECIAL OPERATIONS WING
Hurlburt Field, Florida

352nd SPECIAL OPERATIONS GROUP
RAF Mildenhall, United Kingdom

353rd SPECIAL OPERATIONS GROUP
Kadena AB, Japan

193rd SPECIAL OPERATIONS WING
Harrisburg IAP, Pennsylvania (ANG)

919th SPECIAL OPERATIONS WING
Duke Field, Florida (AFRC)

720th SPECIAL TACTICS GROUP
Hurlburt Field, Florida

USAF SPECIAL OPERATIONS SCHOOL
Hurlburt Field, Florida

18th FLIGHT TEST SQUADRON
Hurlburt Field, Florida

AFSOC AIR SUPPORT OPERATIONS SQUADRON
Forth Bragg, North Carolina

AFRC

The AFRC supports the activity of the active-duty force (ACC, AMC, AFSOC), providing several missions like fighter, bomber, airlift, aerial refuelling. It also provides support to national counterdrug activity and to disaster relief.
The AFRC operates F-16, B-52, A/OA-10, C-5, C-141, C-130, KC-135, HC-130, WC-130, HH-60 aircraft distributed between 36 flying Wings.

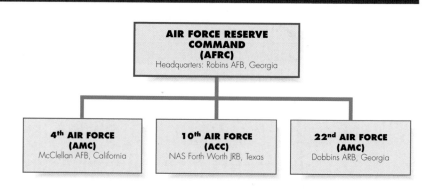

AIR FORCE RESERVE COMMAND (AFRC)
Headquarters: Robins AFB, Georgia

4th AIR FORCE (AMC)
McClellan AFB, California

10th AIR FORCE (ACC)
NAS Forth Worth JRB, Texas

22nd AIR FORCE (AMC)
Dobbins ARB, Georgia

ANG

The ANG provides air defence of Continental US throught the 1st Air Force of ACC. It provides forces and supports activities to active-duty Commands (ACC, AMC, PACAF, AETC, AFSOC) in wartime and during international operations and exercises.
In national emergencies, the ANG units operate under federal government to enforce federal authority, suppress insurrection, and serve in the national defence. In other emergencies, the

AIR NATIONAL GUARD (ANG)
Headquarters: Washington D.C.

ANG units operate under the control of the states governors, especially for disaster relief.
The ANG is formed by 88 Wings present in all the states. It operates F-15, F-16, A/OA-10, B-1, C-5, C-141, C-130, KC-135, EC-130, HC-130, HH-60, plus other aircraft.

USAF FIELD OPERATING AGENCIES

AIR FORCE AUDIT AGENCY

AIR FORCE BASE CONVERSION AGENCY

AIR FORCE CENTER FOR ENVIRONMENTAL EXCELLENCE

AIR FORCE CENTER FOR QUALITY AND MANAGEMENT INNOVATION

AIR FORCE CIVIL ENGINEER SUPPORT AGENCY

AIR FORCE COMMUNICATIONS AGENCY

AIR FORCE COST ANALYSIS AGENCY

AIR FORCE FLIGHT STANDARDS AGENCY

AIR FORCE FREQUENCY MANAGEMENT AGENCY

AIR FORCE HISTORICAL RESEARCH AGENCY

AIR FORCE HISTORY SUPPORT OFFICE

AIR FORCE INSPECTION AGENCY

AIR FORCE LEGAL SERVICES AGENCY

AIR FORCE LOGISTIC MANAGEMENT AGENCY

AIR FORCE MEDICAL OPERATIONS AGENCY

AIR FORCE MEDICAL SUPPORT AGENCY

AIR FORCE NEWS AGENCY

AIR FORCE OFFICE OF SPECIAL INVESTIGATIONS

AIR FORCE OPERATIONS GROUP

AIR FORCE PENTAGON COMMUNICATIONS AGENCY

AIR FORCE PERSONNEL CENTER

AIR FORCE PERSONNEL OPERATIONS AGENCY

AIR FORCE PROGRAM EXECUTIVE OFFICER

AIR FORCE REAL ESTATE AGENCY

AIR FORCE REVIEW BOARDS AGENCY

AIR FORCE SAFETY CENTER

AIR FORCE SECURITY POLICE AGENCY

AIR FORCE SERVICES AGENCY

AIR FORCE STUDIES AND ANALYSIS AGENCY

AIR FORCE TECHNICAL APPLICATIONS CENTER

AIR INTELLIGENCE AGENCY

AIR RESERVE PERSONNEL CENTER

AIR WEATHER SERVICE

COMBAT RESCUE AGENCY

JOINT SERVICES SURVIVAL, EVASION, RESISTANCE, AND ESCAPE AGENCY

The Field Operating Agencies are parts of the Air Force which work under the operational control of an Headquarter functional manager. The FOA have the same administrative and organizational responsabilities as the major commands, but their missions remain separate.

The USAF in Numbers

72.4 billion US $	*(29% of the Defence budget)*

AIR FORCE PERSONNEL STRENGTH (Total force 1997)

Active-duty	
• Officers	74,445
• Enlisted	302,655
• Cadets	4,000
• Civilian	177,780
Total	**558,880**
National Guard (ANG)	109,178
Reserve (AFRC)	140,138
USAF Total force	**808,196**

USAF FLYING SQUADRONS BY MISSION TYPE

Bomber	10
Fighter	54
Reconnaissance	4
Air refuelling	23
Strategic C&C	1
Tactical C&C	5
Electronic warfare	3
Special operations	16
Tactical air control	9
Weather	-
Rescue	7
Airlift	30
Special mission	2
Air National Guard	**90**
Air Force Reserve	**60**
Total	**314**

USAF INSTALLATIONS

US and possessions	160
Foreign	17
Worldwide total	**177**

Type	Active-duty	ANG	AFRC	Total
A/OA-10	223	101	51	375
B-1	81	14	-	95
B-2	19	-	-	19
B-52	85	-	9	94
C-5	81	13	32	126
C-9	23	-	-	23
C-12	37	-	-	37
C-17	27	-	-	27
C-20	13	-	-	13
C-21	76	4	-	80
C-22	-	3	-	3
C-23	3	-	-	3
C-27	10	-	-	10
C-130	311	242	141	694
C/KC-135	303	224	72	599
C-137	6	-	-	6
C-141	156	18	46	220
E-3	32	-	-	32
E-4	4	-	-	4
E-9	2	-	-	2
EC-18	6	-	-	6
EF-111	37	-	-	37
F-4	12	-	-	12
F-15	621	116	-	737
F-16	809	631	73	1513
F-117	57	-	-	57
G-3	3	-	-	3
G-4	14	-	-	14
G-7	9	-	-	9
G-9	4	-	-	4
G-10	1	-	-	1
G-11	2	-	-	2
H-1	70	-	-	70
H-53	46	-	-	46
H-60	58	18	23	99
KC-10	59	-	-	59
SR-71	3	-	-	3
T-1	156	-	-	156
T-3	112	-	-	112
T-37	420	-	-	420
T-38	451	-	-	451
T-39	3	-	-	3
T-41	3	-	-	3
U-2	35	-	-	35
UV-18	2	-	-	2
VC-25	2	-	-	2
Total	**4.499**	**1.426**	**447**	**6.372**

F-15 EAGLE

Air superiority fighter (**F-15A/B/C/D/**) and long range interdiction and air superiority multi-role fighter (**F-15E**). It is utilised by ACC, USAFE, PACAF, AETC, and the ANG. Five different variants are currently in service. The F-15A (and the corresponding F-15B two seat) entered service in 1974, and were followed in 1979 by the F-15C and D models, characterised by increased internal fuel storage and the ability to accept conformal fuel tanks (CFT). Today the F-15A/B are only used by the ANG. From 1985, the air-superiority F-15 have been upgraded to MISP standard (Multistage Improvement Programme), with the APG-63 radar being updated to APG-70 Standard, an improved principal computer, Programmable Armament Control Set, allowing the possibility to deploy AIM-120 AMRAAM missiles, and a new passive electronics defence suite. During the Gulf War the type obtained 36 out of the 39 USAF air-combat victories.

The F-15E Strike Eagle entered service in 1988, and is also capable of performing low level attack missions in all weathers or at night. It is CFT-equipped, with enhanced avionics, and can carry up to 11,120kg of munitions.

CHARACTERISTICS F-15C (*F-15E*)

Constructor: McDonnell Douglas.
Dimensions: wing span 13.05m (42ft 9in); length 19.45m (63ft 9in); height 5.63m (18ft 5.5in); wing area 56.49m².
Weights: empty 12,975kg (28,600lb) - *14,515kg (32,000lb);* maximum take-off weight 30,844kg (68,000lb) - *36,740kg (81,000lb).*
Engines: two Pratt & Whitney F100-PW-220 turbofans each producing 10,646kg *(two Pratt & Whitney F100-PW-229 turbofans each producing 13,211kg 29,100lb).*
Performance: maximum speed Mach 2.5; service ceiling 18,290m (60,000ft), maximum range 5,740km (3,094nm).
Armament: one Vulcan M61A1 20mm cannon, eight Air-to-Air missiles (mix of AIM-9, AIM-7, and AIM-120); the F-15E can additionally carry 11,120kg (24,500lb) of bombs or missiles.
Crew: 1-2 *(2).*

F-15 E

F-16 FIGHTING FALCON

Multi-role fighter. Used by ACC, USAFE, PACAF, AETC, AFRC, and the ANG. Also used by the USAF Acrobatic Team, "The Thunderbirds". The **F-16A** (and the two-seat **B**) entered service in 1979, while deliveries of the **F-16C/D** models began in 1984, which feature improved radar, avionics, engine, and weapons capability. The Block 50 C/D possess a Westinghouse APG-68 radar, wide angle HUD, AMRAAM and HARM missile capability, LANTIRN pods for navigation and attack, GPS, digital flying controls. advanced passive defence systems, and offer the choice of Pratt & Whitney F100-PW-229 or General Electric F110-GE-129 engines. The F-16A/B have been almost completely withdrawn from service, together with the **F-16 ADF** variant, which was developed for National Guard.

CHARACTERISTICS F-16C Block 50

Constructor: Lockheed Martin.
Dimensions: wing span 10m (32ft 9in); length 15.03m (49ft 4in); height 5.09m (16ft 8.5in); wing area 27.87m².
Weights: empty weight 8,437kg (19,020lb); maximum take-off weight 19,187kg (42,300lb).
Engine: one General Electric F110-GE-129 turbofan producing 13,160kg (29,000lb).
Performance: maximum speed Mach 2+; service ceiling 15,240m (more than 50,000ft); maximum range more than 3,218km (1,734nm).
Armament: one Vulcan M61A1 20mm cannon; nine weapons points supporting a maximum of 5,443kg (11,996lb) of bombs, missiles, external tanks, and various pods.
Crew: 1-2.

F-16D

F-117A NIGHTHAWK

Fighterbomber in service with ACC. Commenced operational service with the USAF in 1982. The F-117A was the first USAF aircraft to employ low radar signature technology ("Stealth"). Thanks to the special design study of its profile, construction materials, and protective paint, the Nighthawk is capable of "hiding" from many radar systems, and undertakes high precision night attack missions against high priority targets: thus, the first attack on the Bagdad military command structure during the Gulf War was entrusted to the F-117. The aircraft is equipped with mission computer, laser inertial platform, FLIR and DLIR, laser target designator with autotracker, GPS, and laser guided armament, which together offers maximum precision in navigation and attack.

CHARACTERISTICS

Constructor: Lockheed Martin.
Dimensions: wing span 13.2m (43ft 4in); length 20.09m (65ft 11in); height 3.78m (12ft 5in); wing area 84.82m².
Weights: maximum take-off weight 23,814kg (52,500lb).
Engines: two General Electric F404-GE-F1D2 turbojets producing 4,903kg (10,800lb) each.
Performance: maximum speed 1,040km/h (560kts); operational radius at maximum payload 1,111km (598nm).
Armament: up to 2,268kg (5,000lb) of bombs or missiles carried in an internal bay.
Crew: 1.

A/OA-10A THUNDERBOLT II

Fighterbomber for Close Air Support (CAS) and Forward Air Control (FAC). In use with ACC, USAFE, PACAF, AFRC, ANG. The aircraft entered service with the USAF in 1977 as the **A-10A**, and having been assigned the additional FAC role in 1987, adopted the **OA-10A** designation. Its principle characteristic is the presence of the massive Gatling GAU-8A Avenger seven-barrel 30mm rotating cannon, which offers anti-tanks capability. The cockpit is armoured, and under the wings and fuselage eleven attach points can support external loads. During the Gulf War the type performed 8,100 missions, also obtaining the sole cannon-effected air-to-air victory.

CHARACTERISTICS

Constructor: Northrop Grumman (Fairchild Republic).
Dimensions: wing span 17.53m (57ft 6in); length 16.26m (53ft 4in); height 4.47m (14ft 8in); wing area 47m².
Weights: empty weight 12,700kg (28,000lb); maximum take-off weight 23,586kg (52,000lb).
Engines: two General Electric TF34-GE-100 turbofans, producing 4,115kg (9,065lb) each.
Performance: maximum speed (without external stores) 707km/h (381kts); maximum radius of action (A-10A) 763km (411nm).
Armament: one GAU-8A 30mm cannon with 1,174 rounds; up to 7,257kg (16,000lb) warload, including bombs, missiles, rockets, drop tanks, and various types of pods.
Crew: 1.

A/OA-10A

F-117A

B-2A SPIRIT

Strategic bomber used by ACC. Entering USAF service in 1993, the B-2 is an absolutely unique aircraft, equipped with the most advanced technology, above all in the area of low-observability ("Stealth"). Its aerodynamic configuration is more Stealth-advanced than that featured on the F-117. It is characterised by a "Flying-wing" profile, within which are housed the cockpit and engines. A vastly expensive aircraft, only 20 examples have been ordered, the type serving with the 509th Bomb Wing at Whiteman AFB (Missouri). Despite maintaining a nuclear attack capability, the B-2 is an aircraft dedicated to perform first strikes against the principal targets of a potential enemy, opening the way for aircraft with lesser Stealth characteristics.

CHARACTERISTICS

Constructor: Northrop Grumman.
Dimensions: wing span 52.43m (172ft); length 21.03m (69ft); height 5.18m (17ft); wing area 477.52m².
Weights: empty weight between 45,360 and 56,700kg (100,000-125,000lb); maximum take-off weight around 138,340kg (305,000lb).
Engines: four General Electric F118-GE-100 turbofans producing 8,626kg (19,000lb) each.
Performance: maximum speed around Mach 0.8; service ceiling 15,240m (50,000ft); maximum range (with 14,500kg - 32,000lb of bombs) 11,110km (5,988nm).
Armament: up to a maximum 18,145kg (40,000lb) of bombs (up to 20 B61 nuclear weapons or up to 80 conventional 500lb bombs).
Crew: 2.

B-1B LANCER

Strategic bomber used by ACC and ANG. Entering service in 1985, the B-1B was derived from the B-1A programme, which was abandoned in the 1970s. The aircraft has impressive capabilities, in terms of speed, manoeuvrability, and payload. It was designed for medium and low level penetration missions, delivering nuclear and conventional payloads inside hostile territory. Equipped with advanced navigation and attack systems, the B-1 possesses a variable geometry wing which allows optimisation of performance in both the take-off and landing phase and in high speed low level cruise.
An updating programme was launched in 1993, classified CMUP- Conventional Mission Upgrade Programme.

CHARACTERISTICS

Constructor: Rockwell.
Dimensions: wing span(at minimum sweep) 41.66m (136ft 8in), 23.84m - 78ft 2in (at maximum sweep); length 44.42m (147ft); height 10.24m (34ft); wing area 181.16m².
Weights: empty weight 87,090kg (192,000lb); maximum take-off weight 216,363kg (477,000lb).
Engines: four General Electric F101-GE-102 turbofans, producing 13,975kg (30,780lb) each.
Performance: maximum speed Mach 1.2 (966km/h - 520kts at low level); maximum range 12,000km (6,468nm).
Armament: up to a maximum payload of 56,700kg (125,000lb) of bombs and missiles.
Crew: 4.

B-1B

B-52H STRATOFORTRESS

Strategic bomber used by ACC and AFRC. In use since 1957 (the B-52A model), the B-52 is still an important aircraft in the structure of the USAF. Continually subject to updating and improvement programmes, the latest of which being the CMUP programme launched in 1994, the B-52 performed with great success in the Gulf War, and at present their is no talk of the aircraft being retired: there are current plans to re-engine the surviving aircraft. In August 1994, two B-52H of the 2nd BW undertook the first round-the-world bombing mission, delivering over 12 tonnes of bombs on the Kuwaiti desert during a 47-hour training mission.

CHARACTERISTICS

Constructor: Boeing.
Dimensions: wing span 56.39m (185ft); length 49.04m (160ft 11in); height 12.4m (40ft 8in); wing area 371.61m².
Weights: maximum take-off weight more than 221,353kg (488,000lb).
Engines: eight Pratt & Whitney TF33-P-3 turbofans producing 7,718kg (17,000lb) each.
Performance: maximum speed Mach 0.7; service ceiling over 16,720m (55,000ft); maximum range about 16.000km (8,624nm).
Armament: up to a maximum of 22,680kg (49,986lb) of bombs and missiles.
Crew: 5.

B-52H

EF-111A RAVEN

Electronic warfare aircraft. Used only by ACC. Entering service in 1981, the Raven is a development of the F-111 bomber intended to suppress hostile radar systems by using electronic emissions, at long range, and by accompanying attacking forces and "Escort Jamming". It is equipped with around three tonnes of the sophisticated AN/ALQ-99E electronic apparatus (computer, antennae, receivers, transmitters), similar to that carried by the EA-6B of the US Navy, which is destined to perform the mission also for the USAF after the EF-111A retirement, scheduled for 1998.

CHARACTERISTICS

Constructor: Northrop Grumman.
Dimensions: wing span (minimum sweep) 19.2m (63ft), wing span (maximum sweep) 9.73m (31ft 11in); length 23.16m (76ft); height 6.1m (20ft); wing area 48.77m².
Weights: empty weight 25,072kg (55,275lb); maximum take-off weight 40,346kg (88,948lb).
Engines: two Pratt & Whitney TF30-P-103 turbofans producing 9,461kg (19,600lb) each.
Performance: maximum speed Mach 2.2 (2,272km/h - 1,225kts); service ceiling 13,425m (45,000ft); maximum range 3,704km (8,163nm).
Crew: 2.

B-2A

EF-111A

SR-71 BLACKBIRD

Strategic reconnaissance aircraft. Entered service in 1966, the Blackbirds were retired in 1990 and three were assigned to NASA as research tools. In 1995 three examples were re-introduced into service. Designed by Kelly Johnson as a completely new concept, the SR-71 is the fastest operational piloted aircraft in the world, and thanks to in-flight refuelling can perform reconnaissance missions all over the globe. The on-board equipment comprises an ASARS-1 radar and three high resolution television cameras enabled for real time transmission using a data link.

CHARACTERISTICS

Constructor: Lockheed.
Dimensions: wing span 16,94m (55ft 7in); length 32,74m (107ft 5in);height 5,64m (18ft 6in); wing area 167,22m².
Weights: empty weight 27,216kg (60,000lb), Maximum take-off weight 65,771kg (145,000lb).
Engines: two Pratt & Whitney J58 turbojets producing 14,750kg (32,500lb) each.
Performance: maximum speed over Mach 3 (3,220km/h - 1,735kts); service ceiling 25,908m (85,000ft); maximum range 4,798km (2,586nm) at Mach 3.
Crew: 2.

SR-71

U-2R

U-2

Strategic reconnaissance aircraft. In service since 1982, the present U-2 (initially designated TR-1) are derived from the original U-2A of the 1950s, and are all assigned to ACC. From 1992 the aircraft were designated **U-2R** (and **U-2RT** for the two seat training version). Commencing in 1994, the entire fleet was upgraded to **U-2S/ST** standard, which included the installation of new engines - with a subsequent improvement in global performance - and revised mission systems, amongst which is a high definition electro-optical television camera.

CHARACTERISTICS U-2S

Constructor: Lockheed Martin.
Dimensions: wing span 31.39m (103ft); length 19.2m (63ft); height 5.18m (16ft).
Weights: empty weight 8,074kg (18,000lb); maximum take-off weight 18,145kg (40,000lb).
Engine: one General Electric F118-GE-101 turbofan producing 8,626kg (19,000lb).
Performance: maximum cruising speed 692km/h (373kts); service ceiling 27,430m (90,000ft); maximum range 7,050km (3,800nm) or about 15 hours flying.
Crew: 1-2.

C-130 HERCULES

Tactical transport aircraft. In service with ACC, PACAF, USAFE, AFRC, and the ANG. The C-130A model entered service in 1956, and presently the **C-130E/H** dedicated transport version are in use, while the acquisition of the latest and most advanced variant, the **C-130J**, is planned. The entire fleet has undergone several avionics and structural upgrades. The C-130 is one of the most successful programmes in the world, with over 2100 examples being sold in 64 countries throughout 42 years of production. The USAF uses many other specialised versions of the transport variant for a variety of roles; (see **DC-130A/H, LC-130H, MC-130E/H/P, AC-130H/V, WC-130H, JC-130H, EC-130E/H,** and **EC-130**).

CHARACTERISTICS C-130H

Constructor: Lockheed Martin.
Dimensions: wing span 40.41m (132ft 7in); length 29.79m (97ft 9in); height 11.61m (38ft 3in); wing area 162.11m².
Weights: empty weight 34,702kg (76,469lb); maximum take-off weight 79,389kg (175,000lb); maximum payload 19,340kg (46,673lb).
Engines: four Allison T56-A-15LFE turboprops producing 4,508shp each.
Performance: maximum cruising speed 620km/h (334kts); service ceiling 10,058m (33,000ft); maximum range (with 18,143kg - 40,000lb load) 3,602km (1941nm).
Crew: 4.

MC-130E/H COMBAT TALON

Special Operations aircraft. In service with AFSOC, and used for infiltration and extraction of special forces, tactical low level penetration at night or in bad weather, and in-flight refuelling of AFSOC-operated helicopters. These aircraft are fitted with modified cargo ramps, advanced avionics, terrain-following radar, GPS, NVG, HUD, and sophisticated passive defence and electronics countermeasure systems.

CHARACTERISTICS see C-130

MC/HC-130 COMBAT SHADOW

Special Operations aircraft. In service with AFSOC, and principally used for in-flight refuelling missions in support of AFSOC helicopters in operational theatres characterised by a reduced hostile threat. They are equipped with sophisticated avionics suites encompassing both mission and passive defence systems.

CHARACTERISTICS see C-130

MC-130H

MC/HC-130P

C-130H

AC-130H/U SPECTRE

Special Operations aircraft. In service with AFSOC, the AC-130, also known as a "flying gunship", was born out of the experience of the Vietnam War. The Spectre is capable of potent high precision fire support during escort missions, Close Air Support, surveillance, armed reconnaissance, and interdiction. The aircraft is armed with two six barrel rotating Vulcan 20mm cannon, one 40mm cannon, and a 105mm cannon, with highly sophisticated fire control system comprising a digital fire-control computer, and electro-optical (FLIR, LLLTV) target acquisition systems. The U-model is armed with a 25mm Gatling cannon in place of the two Vulcan. Both versions are armoured, and carry advanced navigational equipment, with comprehensive active and passive defence suites.

CHARACTERISTICS see C-130

EC-130

Electronic Warfare aircraft in service with ACC and ANG. Several differing Electronic Versions have been developed from the transport Hercules. Currently in service are the **EC-130E ABCCC**, utilised as a battlefield command and control system, the **EC-130E "Commando Solo"**, able to perform psychological warfare through the use of radio and television transmissions; and the **EC-130H "Compass Call"**, which are used to disturb and render unavailable hostile communications systems.

CHARACTERISTICS see C-130

C-135 VERSIONI SPECIALI

Many examples of the KC-135 have been modified to serve in various special support roles. The **EC-135C/Y** models serve with ACC, PACAF, and USAFE, and are utilised as flying strategic command and control posts, being equipped with numerous communications systems, including satellite. The **EC-135A/E ARIA** are used to monitor experimental activity. The **RC-135S/U/V/W** and the **OC-135B** are dedicated reconnaissance variants.

CHARACTERISTICS see C-135

WC-130H

Meteorological reconnaissance aircraft. In service with AFRC, they are used for monitoring and forecasting the movement of tropical storms. Their flights also include missions into the eyes of cyclones.

CHARACTERISTICS see C-130

E-3B/C SENTRY

Airborne radar platform dedicated to surveillance, command and control of airspace, also known as AWACS (Airborne Warning and Control System). In use since 1978 with ACC and PACAF. The aircraft, derived from the Boeing 707-320B, was designed to be a flying surveillance station capable of controlling air assets, and for C3 (Communications, Command, and Control), with extended range capability, the ability to operate with flexibility in all weathers, and resistant to hostile electronic interference. The principle system is the Westinghouse AN/APY-1 or -2 radar, characterised by the rotating flat circular antenna on top of the fuselage. From a height of 9,145m (30,000ft), the E-3 is able to detect flying targets up to a distance of 400km (215nm). The aircraft is equipped with ESM, ECM, JTIDS, and TADIL-J systems.

CHARACTERISTICS E-3C

Constructor: Boeing.
Dimensions: wing span 44.42m (145ft 9in); length 46.61m (152ft 11in); height 12.73m (42ft 6in).
Weights: maximum take-off weight 151,953kg (334,900lb).
Engines: four Pratt & Whitney TF33-PW-100 turbofans delivering 9,534kg (18,000lb) each.
Performance: maximum speed 853km/h (460kts) service ceiling 12.768m (42,000ft); maximum range 9,260km (4990nm) or 11 hours flying.
Crew: 24.

E-4B

National command and control operations centre, classified NAOC (National Airborne Operations Centre). In service since 1980, and operated by ACC. The aircraft is essentially a Boeing 747 fitted with special electronic command and control systems able to connect the head of state with strategic military commanders or any other entity. It is capable of operating in a post-nuclear environment, and sports a 1,200 kVA electrical system capable of supporting its advanced electronic systems.

CHARACTERISTICS

Constructor: Boeing.
Dimensions: wing span 59.64m (195ft 8in); length 70.66m (152ft 11in); height 19.94m (41ft 9in); wing area 510.95m².
Weights: maximum take-off weight around 363,200kg (800,000lb).
Engines: four General Electric CF6-50E2 turbofans offering 24,400kg (52,500lb) each.
Performance: maximum speed (at 9,154m - 30,000ft) around 960km/h (517 kts); service ceiling over 13,000m (42,600ft); endurance greater than 12 hours.
Crew: 94.

RC-135V

E-3C

E-4B

AC-130U

EC-130H

WC-130H

VC-25A

Presidential aircraft. In use with AMC since 1990, and assigned to the 89th AW at Andrews AFB. Derived from the Boeing 747-200B, the VC-25A "Air Force One" is equipped with the most advanced navigation and communications systems, and can carry up to 70 passengers of the Presidential staff. It is capable of being in-flight refuelled.

CHARACTERISTICS

Constructor: Boeing.
Dimensions: see E-4B.
Weights: maximum take-off weight 364,879kg (803,700lb).
Engines: four General Electric F103-GE-102 turbofans developing 25,764kg (56,750lb) each.
Performance: maximum cruising speed Mach 0.91: maximum range 11,474km (6,185nm).
Crew: 23.

E-8C JOINT STARS

Battlefield surveillance, management, and target acquisition aircraft. In service since 1996 with ACC. Developed from the Boeing 707-300 airframe, the aircraft is operated by the USAF and US Army as the Joint Surveillance and Attack Radar System (J-STARS). It can also be used for post-strike analysis, SEAD, and detection of hostile missile systems. The principle sensor is the Westinghouse Nordern AN/APY-3 radar.

CHARACTERISTICS

Constructor: Northrop Grumman.
Dimensions: wing span 44.42m (145ft 9in); length 46.61m (152ft 11in); height 12.95m (42ft 6in); wing area 283.35m².
Weights: empty weight 77,560kg (171,000lb); maximum take-off weight 152,400kg (335,800lb).
Engines: four Pratt & Whitney JT3D-3B producing 8,172kg each (18,000lb).
Performance: maximum speed Mach 0.84; service ceiling 12,800m (42,000ft); maximum endurance 11 hours.
Crew: 21 - 34.

E-9A

Radar surveillance aircraft developed from the De Havilland DHC-8 Dash-8m srs 100. Serves with the 475th WEG/ACC at Tyndall AFB, and is tasked with monitoring the Gulf Test Range during exercises or experimental activity.

CHARACTERISTICS

Constructor: De Havilland Canada.
Dimensions: wing span 25.60m (85ft); length 22.25m (73ft); height 7.62m (24ft 7in); wing area 54.30m².
Weights: maximum take-off weight 14,982kg (33,000lb).
Engines: two Pratt & Whitney Canada PW120A turboprops developing 1,800 shp each.
Performance: maximum speed around 400km/h (215kts); service ceiling 7,570m (24,800ft); maximum endurance over 5 hours.
Crew: 3

EC-18

Aircraft tasked with the surveillance and control of experimental activity. In service since 1986 with the Edwards AFB Test Centre, the EC-18, another Boeing 707 development, has two variants: the EC-18A ARIA (Advanced Range Instrumentation Aircraft) and EC-18D CMMCA (Cruise Missile Mission Control Aircraft), the latter monitoring tests of US Navy and USAF Cruise Missiles.

CHARACTERISTICS see C-135

E-8C   E-9A

VC-25A

EC-18B

C-5 GALAXY

Long range heavy transport aircraft. Serves with AMC, AFRC, ANG, and AETC. The first examples (C-5A) were delivered to the USAF from 1969. The **C-5B** model entered service in 1986, featuring a reinforced wing, new turbofan engines, and updated avionics. In standard configuration it can accommodate 75 passengers and 36 pallets, or two M60 MBTs, or three CH-47C helicopters, or up to a maximum of 340 passengers in air-bus configuration. Two C-5A were modified to accept oversized loads, and are classified **C-5C**.

CHARACTERISTICS C-5B

Constructor: Lockheed Martin.
Dimensions: wing span 67.88m (222ft 8in); length 75.54m (247ft 10in); height 19.85m (65ft 1in); wing area 575.98m².
Weights: empty weight 169,796kg (374,000lb); maximum take-off weight 379,998kg (837,000lb).
Engines: four General Electric TF39-GE-1C turbofans developing 19,522kg (43,000lb) each.
Performance: maximum speed 917km/h (494kts); service ceiling around 10,860m (35,750ft); maximum range 11,908km (6,470nm).
Crew: 6.

C-141B STARLIFTER

Long range heavy transport aircraft. Used by AMC, AFRC, ANG, and AETC. The first of 285 C-141A was delivered to the USAF in 1965, contributing notably to military operations in Vietnam, but from subsequent studies the C-141B arose, with a fuselage extended by 7.01m (23ft) and capable of being in-flight refuelled. This version began to enter service in 1979. The Starlifter forms the backbone of the USAF's strategic transport capability, and can transport 13 pallets, or 200 equipped soldiers, or 155 paratroopers, or 103 stretchers for evacuation and medical transport.

CHARACTERISTICS

Constructor: Lockheed Martin.
Dimensions: wing span 48.74m (159ft 11in); length 51.29m (168ft 3in); height 11.96m (39ft 3in); wing area 299.88m².
Weights: empty weight 68,100kg (150,090lb); maximum take-off weight 156,584kg (345,100lb).
Engines: four Pratt & Whitney TF33-P-7 turbofans developing 9,534kg (21,000lb) each.
Performance: maximum speed 909km/h (490kts); range (with maximum payload) 4,773km (2,572nm).
Crew: 5

C-17A GLOBEMASTER III

Long range heavy transport aircraft. In service since 1993 with AMC and AFRC. The C-17 is a transport aircraft designed to re-supply and liaise with forces operating at long distances from their home base, with the additional capability of operating, in a tactical scenario, into airfields previously reserved for C-130-type tactical transports. The USAF intends to purchase 120 examples. The C-17 has a maximum payload of 76.726kg (169,100lb), and is the first military transport equipped with full "Fly-by-Wire" controls, four multi-function screens, HUD, and a crew comprising only two pilots and a loadmaster.

CHARACTERISTICS

Constructor: McDonnell Douglas.
Dimensions: wing span 51.76m (169ft 10in); length 53.04m (174ft); height 16.79m (55ft 1in); wing area 353.03m².
Weights: empty weight 122,015kg (268,920lb); maximum take-off weight 265,351kg (584,800lb).
Engines: four Pratt & Whitney F117-PW-100 turbofans producing 18,930kg (40,700lb) each.
Performance: maximum speed Mach 0.87; service ceiling 12,500m (41,000ft); maximum range (with 71,214kg - 156,950lb payload) 4,445km (2,395nm).
Crew: 3.

KC-10A EXTENDER

Long range transport and tanker aircraft. Serves with AMC and AFRC, deliveries having commenced in 1981. Derived from the DC-10 series 30CF airliner, the Extender is able to operate simultaneously as a tanker and cargo transport, directly supporting the re-deployment of forces to distant theatres. The transport capacity can accommodate up to 75 people, and a maximum of 27 supply pallets. the maximum payload is 76,911kg (169,511lb). The KC-10 is fitted with both principle in-flight refuelling systems, enabling it to refuel additionally the aircraft of the US Navy and Marines, and those of the NATO alliance.

CHARACTERISTICS

Constructor: McDonnell Douglas.
Dimensions: wing span 50.42m (165ft 4in); length 55.29m (181ft 7in); height 17.68m (58ft 1in); wing area 364.30m².
Weights: empty weight 121,198kg (267,120lb); maximum take-off weight 267,860kg (590,360lb).
Engines: three General Electric CF6-50C2 turbofans developing 23,835kg (52,500lb) each.
Performance: maximum cruising speed 908km/h (490kts); service ceiling 12,770m (42,000ft); maximum range (with maximum payload) 7,022km (3,785nm).
Crew: 4.

KC-10A

C-5B

C-17A

KC-135 STRATOTANKER

In-flight refuelling and transport aircraft derived from the Boeing 707. In service with AMC, PACAF, USAFE, AFRC, ANG, and AETC, it commenced USAF operations in 1958 (KC-135A), and for the last forty years has formed the backbone of Air Force in-flight-refuelling capacity. Some 550 examples remain active, operating in **KC-135E/R/T** configurations. The fuel tanks are located in the wings and lower fuselage, while the upper section can accept supply pallets or up to eighty passengers. The differing variants in use are distinguished by the engine type installed. Improvement programmes include an avionics upgrade and a Life Extension Structural Modification (LEMS) which will permit the KC-135 to operate until approximately the year 2020.

CHARACTERISTICS KC-135R

Constructor: Boeing.
Dimensions: wing span 39.88m (130ft 10in); length 41m (136ft 3in); height 11.68m (38ft 4in); wing area 226.02m².
Weights: empty weight 54,130kg (119,300lb); maximum take-off weight 146,188kg (322,200lb); transferable fuel load 54,431kg (120,000lb).
Engines: four CFM International F108-CF-100 turbofans delivering 10,089kg (22,220lb) each.
Performance: maximum speed 980km/h (528kts); service ceiling 15,150m (49,700ft); maximum range (with maximum deliverable fuel capacity) 3,420km (1,843nm).
Crew: 4.

C-135 STRATOLIFTER

Long range transport aircraft. In use with ACC, AMC, and PACAF in **C-135A** and **C-135B** versions. The first examples were delivered to the USAF in 1961. The C-135A is substantially a version of the KC-135 without the in-flight refuelling system, and was introduced as a stop gap long range transport prior to the arrival of the C-141. Subsequently, examples of the C-135A/B have been converted into **WC-135B** (for long range weather reconnaissance), **RC-135E/M** (for electronic reconnaissance), and **TC-135S/W**.

CHARACTERISTICS

Constructor: Boeing.
Dimensions: wing span 39.88m (130ft 10in); length 40.4m (134ft 6in); height 11.68m (38ft 4in); wing area 226.02m².
Weights: empty weight 46,444kg (102,360lb); maximum take-off weight 125,077kg (275,670lb).
Engines: four CFM International F108-CF-100 turbofans delivering 10,089kg (22,220lb) each.
Performance: maximum speed 980km/h (528kts); service ceiling 15,150m (49,700ft); maximum range (with 24,516kg - 54,000lb cargo) 7,432km (4,000nm).
Crew: 4.

C-137 STRATOLINER

IP transport aircraft operated by AMC. There are four **C-137C** (Boeing 707-320) and one **C-137B** (Boeing 707-120). Two of the C variants were previously used as "Air Force One", the aircraft used to transport the President of the United States.

CHARACTERISTICS C-137C

Constructor: Boeing.
Dimensions: wing span 44.42m (145ft 9in); length 46.61m (152ft 11in); height 12.93m (42ft 5in); wing area 283.35m².
Weights: empty weight 66,400kg (146,340lb); maximum take-off weight 151,320kg (333,500lb).
Engines: four Pratt & Whitney JT3D-3 turbofans producing 7,808kg (17,200lb) each.
Performance: maximum speed 1,007km/h (543kts); service ceiling 12,700m (41,700ft); maximum range 8,276km (4,460nm).

C-27A SPARTAN

Tactical transport. Utilised by ACC at Howard AFB; deliveries began in 1991. The Spartan is derived from the STOL Alenia G.222 transport, modified by Chrysler with new avionics systems, and is used to carry cargo and personnel into theatres where only semi-prepared strips are available. It can carry up to 34 fully equipped troops or up to a maximum payload of 6,742kg (14,860lb) of supplies.

CHARACTERISTICS

Constructor: Alenia.
Dimensions: wing span 28.7m (94ft 2in); length 22.7m (74ft 5in); height 10.57m (34ft 8in); wing area 82m².
Weights: empty weight 15,700kg (34,600lb); maximum take-off weight 25,800kg (56,900lb).
Engines: two General Electric T64-P4D turboprops producing 3,400shp each.
Performance: maximum speed 487km/h (262kts); service ceiling 7,600m (25,000ft); maximum range (with maximum payload) 1,259km (678nm).
Crew: 3.

C-135A

C-137

KC-135E

C-27A

C-9 NIGHTINGALE

Medical transport aircraft. In service with AMC and AFRC. The first aircraft were delivered in 1968. Derived from the Douglas DC-9 srs 30, the **C-9A** features a special internal configuration enabling the transport of 40 stretcher patients and five accompanying medical staff. Several aircraft are detached to Europe and the Pacific. Three **C-9C** with a special configuration are assigned to the 89th AW for transport of Government personnel.

CHARACTERISTICS C-9A

Constructor: McDonnell Douglas.
Dimensions: wing span 28.47m (93ft 3in); length 38.28m (119ft 3in); height 8.53m (27ft 6in); wing area 92.97m².
Weights: maximum take-off weight 49,032kg (108,000lb).
Engines: two Pratt & Whitney JT8D-9 turbofans producing 6,583kg (14,500lb) each.
Performance: maximum cruising speed 907km/h (490kts); service ceiling 10,605m (35,000ft); maximum range more than 3,215km (1,733nm).
Crew: 3.

C-12 HURON

Light transport aircraft. In service with AMC, PACAF, and ANG, the C-12 are the military versions of the Beechcraft Super King Air 200, and are used in support of military missions and attaches throughout the world, and for transport and training within the USA. The early **C-12A** were re-engined with Pratt & Whitney PT6A-41 turboprops, and re-designated **C-12C**. **C-12D** and **F** models are also in service. Up to eight passengers or 2,162kg (4,765lb) of freight can be carried.

CHARACTERISTICS C-12F

Constructor: Raytheon (Beechcraft).
Dimensions: wing span 16.61m (54ft 6in); length 13.34m (43ft 9in); height 4.57m (15ft); wing area 28.15m².
Weights: empty weight 3,791kg (8,358lb); maximum take-off weight 5,670kg (12,500lb).
Engines: two Pratt & Whitney PT6A-42 turboprops producing 850shp each.
Performance: maximum speed 544km/h (294kts); service ceiling 10,688m (35,000ft); maximum range 3,746km (2,023nm).
Crew: 2.

C-20 GULFSTREAM

VIP transport aircraft. In service since 1983, they are used by AMC and USAFE for SAM operations (Special Airlift Mission). Initially **C-20A** and **B** models were acquired, derived from the civilian Gulfstream III, and capable of carrying a maximum of eighteen passengers. Successive acquisitions were the military version of the Gulfstream IV, the **C-20H**.

CHARACTERISTICS C-20H

Constructor: Gulfstream.
Dimensions: wing span 23.72m (77ft 10in); length 26.92m (88ft 4in); height 7.44m (24ft 5in); wing area 88.26m².
Weights: empty weight 16,100kg (35,500lb); maximum take-off weight 33,838kg (74,600lb).
Engines: two Rolls Royce Tay Mk.611-8 turbofans delivering 6,288kg (13,850lb) each.
Performance: maximum speed Mach 0.88; service ceiling 13,715m (45,000ft) ; maximum range (with 8 passengers) 7,815km (4,220nm).
Crew: 5.

C-21A

Light transport aircraft. In service since 1984, and assigned to AMC, PACAF, and USAFE. The C-21A is a military version of the Learjet 35A, and is utilised for the rapid transport of personnel and supplies in the Pacific, European, and Continental US theatres. It can carry up to eight passengers of 1,431kg (3,154lb) of freight, and can also operate as a medical transport.

CHARACTERISTICS

Constructor: Learjet.
Dimensions: wing span 12.04m (39ft 6in); length 14.83m (48ft 8in); height 3.76m (12ft 3in); wing area 23.53m².
Weights: empty weight 4,590kg (10,120lb); maximum take-off weight 8.300kg (18,300lb).
Engines: two Alliedsignal TFE731-2 turbofans developing 1,589kg (3,500lb) each.
Performance: maximum speed 870km/h (470kts); service ceiling 12,423m (40,800ft); maximum range (with 4 passengers) 4,067km (2,192nm).
Crew: 2.

C-9A

C-21A

C-12C

C-20A

C-22B

Passenger transport aircraft.
In service with the ANG, the **C-22B** is the military version of the Boeing 727, and has 90 seats arranged into two classes. Two aircraft were modified to accommodate increased fuel, and to operate with higher landing weights.

CHARACTERISTICS

Constructor: Boeing.
Dimensions: wing span 32.92m (108ft); length 46.69m (153ft); height 10.36m (34ft); wing area 157.93m².
Weights: empty weight 46,675kg (102,870lb); maximum take-off weight 95,000kg (209,380lb).
Engines: three Pratt & Whitney JT8D turbofans producing 6,570kg (14,480lb) each.
Performance: maximum speed 999km/h (538kts); maximum range over 4,000km (2,156nm).

C-23A SHERPA

Tactical transport aircraft.
Three aircraft operated by AFMC at Edwards AFB for the AFFTC. A military version of the Shorts 330, the C-23 entered service with the USAFE in 1984, and was subsequently re-assigned to the National Guard.

CHARACTERISTICS

Constructor: Shorts.
Dimensions: wing span 22.76m (74ft 8in); length 17.69m (58ft); height 4.95m (16ft 3in); wing area 42.08m².
Weights: empty weight 6,680kg (14,723lb); maximum take-off weight 11,577kg (25,500lb).
Engines: two Pratt & Whitney Canada PT6A-45R turboprops producing 1,198shp each.
Performance: maximum cruising speed 350km/h (188kts); maximum range (with 2,270kg - 5,000lb of freight) 1,237km (666nm).
Crew: 3.

HH-1H IROQUOIS

Multi-role transport helicopter.
Derived from the civil Bell 205, it entered USAF service in 1970. Originally ordered as a rescue helicopter, it is used today by Air Force Space Command (AFSPC) for liaison and support between missile bases. The HH-1H can carry up to 12 passengers or 1,089kg (2,400lb) of freight.

CHARACTERISTICS

Constructor: Bell.
Dimensions: length with rotors running 17.62m (57ft); main rotor diameter 14.63m (48ft); height 4.6m (15ft).
Weights: empty weight 2,400kg (5,290lb); maximum take-off weight 4,313kg (9,505lb).
Engine: one Textron Lycoming T53-L-13B turbine delivering 1,400shp.
Performance: maximum speed 193km/h (104kts); service ceiling 4,075m (13,370ft); maximum range 557km (300nm).
Crew: 2.

UH-1N IROQUOIS

Multi-role transport helicopter.
Derived from the civilian Bell 212, itself substantially a twin-engined development of the 205, the UH-1N entered USAF service in 1970. Today it is used by AFSPC and PACAF for liaison and support, and by AFSOC for training duties. It can transport up to 14 passengers or 1,816kg (4,000lb) of cargo.

CHARACTERISTICS

Constructor: Bell.
Dimensions: length with rotors running 17.46m (57ft); main rotor diameter 14.69m (48ft); height 4.53m (14ft).
Weights: empty weight 2,786kg (6,140lb); maximum take-off weight 5,080kg (11,200lb).
Engines: two Pratt & Whitney Canada T400-CP-400 producing 1,290shp each.
Performance: maximum speed 230km/h (124kts); service ceiling 4,330m (14,200ft); maximum range 420km (226nm).
Armament (*optional*)**:** two General Electric 7.62mm miniguns and two 40mm grenade launchers; two seven tube 2.75" rocket launchers.
Crew: 2.

MH-53J PAVE LOW III

Special duties rescue and transport helicopter. In use since 1987, the **MH-53J** is an update of the MH-53H, HH/CH-53B/C models for use with AFSOC. The Pave Low III is intended for the infiltration into and extraction from hostile territory of combat units of the Special Forces, and can operate both at night and in bad weather: it is also used for Combat-SAR. It is equipped with both sophisticated navigation systems (TF/TA AN/APQ-158 radar, FLIR, GPS, NVG, Doppler) and active and passive defence systems (AN/ALQ-162 ACM/ECCM, ALQ-157, ALE-40, ALR-69, AAR-47), an in-flight refuelling boom, armour, and machine guns. Six **TH-53A** also serve in the training role.

CHARACTERISTICS

Constructor: Sikorsky.
Dimensions: length with rotors running 30.18m (99ft); main rotor diameter 24.08m (79ft); height 5.66m (18ft 6in).
Weights: empty weight around 16,000kg (35,200lb); maximum take-off weight around 22,700kg (50,000lb).
Engines: three General Electric T64-GE-100 turbines delivering 4,330shp each.
Performance: maximum speed 315km/h (170kts); service range 5,659km (3,050nm).
Armament: Colt-Browning 12.7mm machine guns and 7.62mm Miniguns.
Crew: 6.

C-23A

MH-53J

C-22B

UH-1N

MH/HH-60G PAVE HAWK

Special duties transport and rescue helicopter. In service with AFSOC (**MH-60G**) for operational support of Special Forces, and with ACC, PACAF, AFRC, and ANG (**HH-60G**) for Combat-SAR. The helicopters are equipped with sophisticated navigation equipment, and active and passive defence systems for night and/or bad-weather missions over hostile territory, they also possess an in-flight refuelling probe.

CHARACTERISTICS

Constructor: Sikorsky
Dimensions: length with rotors running 19.76m (65ft); main rotor diameter 16.36m (53ft 8in); height 5.13m (16ft 10in).
Weights: empty weight 4,823kg (10,630lb); maximum take-off weight 10,215kg (22,500lb).
Engines: two General Electric T700-GE-700/701C turbines producing 1,560shp each.
Performance: maximum speed 356km/h (192kts); service ceiling 5,757m (18,900ft); maximum range 803km (433nm).
Armament: 7.62mm Minigun and a 12.7mm machine gun (only on MH-60G).
Crew: 3-4.

T-1A JAYHAWK

Trainer. Serving with AETC since 1992, the T-1A is used for advanced training for pilots destined to multi-engined types. The aircraft is a derivative of the Beechjet 400A, structurally strengthened, with advanced avionics and additional fuel tank in the fuselage. The USAF has ordered 180 examples.

CHARACTERISTICS

Constructor: Raytheon (Beechcraft).
Dimensions: wing span 13.26m (43ft 6in); length 14.76m (48ft 5in); height 4.24m (13ft 11in); wing area 22.43m².
Weights: empty weight 4,558kg (10,000lb); maximum take-off weight 7,303kg (16,100lb).
Engines: two Pratt & Whitney Canada JT15D-5B turbofans delivering 1,316kg (2,900lb) each.
Performance: maximum speed 864km/h (465kts); service ceiling 13,715m (45,000ft); maximum range 3,570km (1,924nm).
Crew: 3.

T-3A FIREFLY

Selection aircraft and basic trainer. In service with the AETC and the Air Force Academy since 1993, and used to select and grade potential pilots prior to the beginning of main training. It is derived from the Slingsby T67m-260 Firefly.

CHARACTERISTICS

Constructor: Slingsby.
Dimensions: wing span 10.59m (34ft 9in); length 7.55m (24ft 10in); height 2.36m (7ft 9in); wing area 12.63m².
Weights: empty weight 794kg (1,780lb); maximum take-off weight 1,145kg (2,520lb).
Engine: one Textron Lycoming AEIO-540-D4A5 260hp piston engine.
Performance: maximum speed 281km/h (151kts); service ceiling 5,757m (18,900ft); maximum range 753km (405nm).
Crew: 1-2.

T-37B TWEET

Primary training aircraft. In service with the USAF since 1959, and assigned to AETC and AMC. Around 420 T-37B remain active, having been submitted to a SLEP programme by Sabreliner, comprising a modification package that will extend the type's useful life beyond 2000. It will be replaced by the winner of the JPATS competition, the Raytheon Beech Mk.II, a derivative of the Pilatus PC-9.

CHARACTERISTICS

Constructor: Cessna.
Dimensions: wing span 10.93m (33ft 9in); length 8.62m (29ft 3in); height 2.71m (9ft 2in); wing area 17.98m².
Weights: empty weight 1,757kg (3,870lb); maximum take-off weight 2,985kg (6,575lb).
Engines: two Continental J69-T-25 producing 465kg (1,025lb) each.
Performance: maximum speed 685km/h (370kts); service ceiling 10,635m (34,900ft); maximum range 1,398km (753nm).
Crew: 1-2.

T-38 TALON

Advanced training aircraft. Delivered to the USAF from 1961, the **T-38A** was derived from the lightweight F-5A fighter, from which it inherits its general performance and supersonic capability. Over 370 T-38A remain in service, above all with AETC. The **AT-38B** model is the armed version of the Talon, featuring a gunsight in the cockpit and a ventral munitions pylon: it is used for advanced IFF training (Introduction to Fighter Fundamentals). The Pacer Classic programme, a modification and upgrading kit, will extend the life of the T-38 until 2020.

CHARACTERISTICS

Constructor: Northrop.
Dimensions: wing span 7.70m (25ft 3in); length 14.13m (29ft 3in); height 3.92m (9ft 2in); wing area 15.80m².
Weights: empty weight 3,252kg (7,165lb); maximum take-off weight 5,465kg (12,093lb).
Engines: two General Electric J85-GE-5A turbojets producing 1,748kg (3,850lb) each.
Performance: maximum speed Mach 1.23: service ceiling 16,335m (53,500ft); maximum range 1,756km (946nm).
Crew: 1-2.

HH-60G

T-37B

T-1A

T-3A

T-38A

T-43A

Navigation training aircraft.
In service with the USAF since 1973, and operated by AETC and the ANG. Equipped with radar, stellar, and inertial navigation systems, LORAN, and varied radio-aids, the T-43A has 17 navigator training stations, plus three for the instructors. The T-43 is a derivative of the Boeing 737-200: two examples have been converted to VIP transports, and are designated **CT-43**.

CHARACTERISTICS

Constructor: Boeing.
Dimensions: wing span 28.35m (93ft); length 30.53m (100ft); height 11.28m (37ft); wing area 91.04m^2.
Weights: empty weight 27,692kg (61,000lb); maximum take-off weight 52,437kg (115,500lb).
Engines: two Pratt & Whitney JT8D-9 turbofans producing 6,583kg (14,500lb) each.
Performance: maximum speed 943km/h (508kts); service ceiling around 10,600m (34,800ft); maximum range 4,813km (2,595nm).
Crew: 2.

UV-18B TWIN OTTER

Transport and para-drop aircraft. Two examples are operated since 1977 by the Air Force Academy to support cadet parachute training.
The UV-18 is the military version of the De Havilland DHC-6 Twin Otter, and can carry up to 20 passengers.

CHARACTERISTICS

Constructor: De Havilland Canada.
Dimensions: wing span 19.81m (65ft); length 15.77m (51ft 9in); height 5.94m (19ft 6in); wing area 39.02m^2.
Weights: empty weight 3,363kg (7,400lb); maximum take-off weight 5,670kg (12,500lb).
Engines: two Pratt & Whitney Canada PT6A-27 turboprops producing 620shp each.
Performance: maximum cruising speed 338km/h (182kts); service ceiling 8,140m (26,700ft); maximum range (with 1,134kg - 2,500lb of cargo) 1,297km (700nm).
Crew: 2.

QF-106A/B

The OF-106 is a radio-controlled flying target version of the F-106 Delta Dart interceptor. Around 194 of the F-106A and two-seat F-106B were brought up to QF-106 FSAT standard (Full Scale Aerial Target) by Honeywell, using GRDCUS, DFCS, and DTCS guidance systems, serving with ACC at Tyndall and Holloman AF Bases. The QF-106 will retire from service during 1997.

CHARACTERISTICS

Constructor: Convair.
Dimensions: wing span 11.67m (38ft 5in); length 21.56m (70ft 8in); height 6.18m (20ft 3in); wing area 58.65m^2.
Weights: empty weight 10,728kg (23,640lb); maximum operational weight 18,387kg (40,525lb).
Engine: one Pratt & Whitney J75-P-17 turbojet delivering 11,113kg (24,500lb).
Performance: maximum speed at 12,190m (40,000ft) 2,454km/h (mach 2.31): service ceiling 17,385m (57,000ft); maximum range 1,173km (632nm).
Crew: 1-2.

QF-4

The QF-4 is replacing the QF-106 as the standard USAF FSAT aircraft. Derived from the multi-role F-4 Phantom fighter, the QF-4 is converted by Tracor into a target aircraft using the installation of GRDCUS, DFCS, and NGTCS systems. Around 300 Phantoms will be converted to radio controlled target standard.

CHARACTERISTICS QF-4E

Constructor: McDonnell Douglas.
Dimensions: wing span 11.68m (38ft 5in); length 19.20m (63ft); height 5.03m (16ft 5in); wing area 49.24m^2.
Weights: empty weight 13,770kg (30,350lb); maximum operational weight 22,473kg (49,530lb).
Engines: two General Electric J79-GE-17 turbojets delivering 8,119kg (17,000lb) each.
Performance: maximum speed (at 12,200m - 40,000ft) 2,390km/h (1,288kts)(Mach 2.25); service ceiling 18,975m (62,200ft); radius of action 958km (516nm).
Crew: 1-2.

QF-106A

T-43A

QF-4

UV-18B

OTHER AIRCRAFT IN SERVICE
(used by the Air Force Academy)

TG-3A	(SGS 1-26E)	GLIDER
TG-4A	(SGS 2-33A)	GLIDER
TG-7A	(SGM 237)	GLIDER
TG-9A	(ASK-21)	GLIDER
TG-11A	(SGM 237)	MOTORIZED GLIDER

A GLIMPSE AT THE FUTURE

*I*n a world in which innovation is constantly in progress, a structure featured by top technology as the USAF is never resting, but on the contrary, through its numerous units and laboratories devoted to research and testing, often team-working with the industries, it stands between the bodies capable to conceive and realise itself innovation. So, the Air Force has always several new project in phase of definition, development or test, as to always have the best equipments available.

Between the numerous programs which have been developing at the end of this Century, we mention the new air superiority "superfighter", the Lockheed-Boeing F-22A, which will replace the F-15 from the year 2004; the new multirole combat fighter, the *Joint Strike Fighter* (JSF), which should replace the F-16 before 2010; the new JPATS turboprop trainer *Beech-Pilatus Mk.II*, whose introduction in service is scheduled for 1999; the revolutionary tiltrotor Bell-Boeing CV-22 *Osprey*, destined to be operated by AFSOC in lieu of the MH-53 helicopter from 2003; the new series of Unmanned Aerial Vehicles (UAV), destined to perform some strategic and tactical reconnaissance missions: the Tier II *Predator*, the Tier II *Plus Global Hawk*, and the Tier III *Minus DarkStar*, of which only the first is operational since the end of 1996.

Other projects are under development, as the AirBorne Laser (ABL), a high-power laser system carried on board of a Boeing 747-400F to intercept and destroy ICBMs at great distance from their targets. Others again, more advanced and sophisticated, are in the definition phase.

Global Engagement is the new Air Force doctrine for the 21st Century. As Secretary of the Air Force dr. Sheila E. Widnall says, "Global Engagement is air and space power that covers all aspects of the Air Force – people, capabilities and support structures. It charts a path into the next century as an Air Force team within a joint team. It is our continuing commitment to provide America the air and space capabilities to deter, fight and win".

NOTES ABOUT AUTHOR AND PHOTOS

Riccardo Niccoli was born in Florence in 1961. He earned a degree in Political Science and works as free-lance jounalist and photographer. Since 1982, he has been publishing articles and photos on some of the most important European aviation magazines. In Italy, he is contributor to the aviation magazines "Volare", published by the Editoriale Domus, and to "Rivista Aeronautica", officially published by the Italian Air Force. Privat pilot and ex-parachutist officer, he is author also of other aviation books.
He lives in Novara with his wife Lucia and his son Federico.

The author usually works with two 35mm reflex autofocus cameras, and a series of lenses ranging from the wide-angle 17mm to the telephoto 300mm lens, sometimes increased by the use of a 1.6x teleconverter. The films used have been mainly of the 64 and 100 ISO slides type. All the photos in this book have been taken with absolutely standard materiel, without any technical modification to the cameras, or special films and filters, even during the in-flight sessions.

The images appearing in this book have been realised thanks to numerous reportages carried out at USAF airbases during exercises, normal training activity, and air shows in the past few years; they have been selected between a total of more than 8,000 slides taken on the ground and in-flight.

ACKNOWLEDGMENTS

The author wishes to thank Gen. Ronald R. Fogleman, USAF Chief of Staff, Gen. Donald W. Shepperd, Air National Guard Director, all the Air Force personnel, and especially the PAO of the ACC, the AMC, the ANG, the Golden Air Tatoo at Nellis AFB, and of the single bases visited, the personnel of the USIA in Washington D.C. and that of the USIS at the US Embassy in Rome: without their support and cooperation this book would have not been published.
A special thanks is also for Frank McMeiken, who took charge of the text translation into English.